Here Lies America: 1776-2016

Larry Stewart

Copyright © 2024

Larry Stewart

ISBN

All Rights Reserved. Any unauthorized reprint or use of this material is strictly prohibited. No part of this book may be reproduced or transmitted in any form or by any means, electronic or mechanical, including photocopying, recording, or by any information storage and retrieval system without express written permission from the author.

All reasonable attempts have been made to verify the accuracy of the information provided in this publication. Nevertheless, the author assumes no responsibility for any errors and/or omissions.

For my best friend and wife Jo Ann! For putting up with me all these years. I love you!

Table of Contents

Preface i
Beans, meat, and ale 1
State of dis-union 9
Shrinkies 12
Boston 14
Pie and Blood 17
Philly Steak 20
Just a swingin' 22
The Senator 25
Philadelphia 38
Kentucky calling 41
New York 44
Zombies, Wildcats, and maggots… Oh my! 48
Went to a garden party 52
New York 56
Washington 57
Bill and Larry 59
Stones and bullets 60
A star is born 62
Let it snow 64
More things go missing 69
Washington notices 70

The warning	73
Back to Kentucky	75
The Senator from Kentucky	78
Audience with the President	80
The flight	85
A decision	88
The Pastor tells all	90
The Deal	94
Back to Washington	96
Feathers and Tea	97
Fox, CNN, and MSNBC – Oh my!	99
The joint session	105
Washington speaks to the people	109
6.5 Boston	112
6.5 Washington	115
The Mall	118
The Fears of a clown	120
The edge of revolution	130
Ashton	132
Changes to be made?	133
The last attempt	134
Jan 21, 2016	138
A President in Peril	141
It came to a Shore	144

Washington – Gone!	146
Philadelphia – Gone!	147
Boston – Gone!	148
Norfolk – Gone!	149
Back in Kentucky	150
The last dream?	153
Louisville, KY	161
The new kids on the block	163
Aftermath	165
Off-limits	168
Stuff and things	172

Preface

I write this book as a concerned citizen of the United States of America, a citizen who feels his freedom of speech has been silenced and that his right to an opinion has been curb-stomped. I recently sent emails to the two Senators from my state, asking about things that concerned me, not expecting a response. I did, however, get a response within a week from one of them. The other, a few months later, told me thanks for my letter and they would get back to me, but they never did.

This is part of the response from the Senator, who *seemed* to care and gave me some hope for our future. Read it and see what you think. Then please continue the book which all came to my mind. I am a history buff and just used whatever popped into my head with a few facts from the Internet. Any resemblance to my friends and family is on purpose, and I hope you don't mind. I love you guys!

The Senator replied……

We have also witnessed several troubling instances of misdirection and misrepresentation of facts on the part of senior Administration officials. These numerousscandals – the improper targeting of certain

Conservative groups by the Internal Revenue Service, the failed government-run gun trading operation known as "Fast and Furious," the subpoena of journalists' phone records by the Department of Justice, the unconstitutional gathering of electronic communications by the National Security Agency, and the misleading of the American public as to the true nature of the attack on our diplomatic facility in Benghazi, Libya – deserve much more scrutiny than they have yet received.

I believe that these episodes are symptoms of a much more fundamental problem that we face as a nation: an arrogant federal government that has simply grown too large, too invasive, too distant from people, and utterly adrift from its Constitutional moorings. As I have often said, Big Government is *not* your friend. It is impossible to trust a government that does not respect the Constitution, does not cooperate fully with Congressional oversight, and goes to such great lengths to keep the public in the dark.

However, we must not become so discouraged by the problems of the present that we simply give up on shaping a better future. At my swearing-in as a UnitedStates Senator, I took an oath to protect and defend the Constitution, and I take that responsibility very seriously. Eternal vigilance is the price of liberty; rest assured that as long as I am in office, I will continue to vigorously defend the rights of all Americans and I willfight to restore the limits placed on the federal government by the Constitution.

Sounds to me that at least someone took the time to respond to each of my points. It gives me some hope that this great nation can become great again. If what I have written here offends you, too bad. It is my opinion, and I am allowed by my Constitutional Rights to have one of those. It might be if you read these thoughts and think someone or something resembles you. If you are looking for a book with big fancy words, you won't find it here.

A special thanks to all of the men and women who have served or are serving this great nation. Thanks, and GOD Bless America!

LW.

Beans, meat, and ale

The wet grass made a light, slippery noise as his men made their way through the dense thicket, up the hill to where the Redcoats had set up encampment three days earlier. The morning dew was rising slowly up from the ground to create an eerie feeling that already added to the nervousness of the situation.

The only sound was that of the few dozen men making their way to what was sure to be certain death or capture. The tops of the trees looked like dark, ominous spirits looking down on their next victim. This was normal for an early February morning in Massachusetts.

The King's army was tough to beat, the best-trained army in the world. Many of them had made a three-month trip across the ocean to quell the rebellion. They did not want to be here. The rugged terrain did not suit their type of warfare, and the Continental Army was starting to use this to its advantage.

Adding to the British war woes was the fact that supplies and reinforcements took even longer than the initial voyage westward. There were times when stealing had become necessary to feed the soldiers. Some of the local citizens, still loyal to the crown, had offered up food and supplies. Those who didn't usually have it taken anyway.

It was difficult to know who to trust; many of those loyal

to the rebellion operated in secrecy, much like those pesky Sons of Liberty from the Boston area. The Sons made it a habit to interrupt British operations, and rumor has it they were local men of prestige and wealth who had nothing better to do.

It was no better for the Colonials either. Food, weapons, ammunition, and uniforms, especially shoes, were in short supply. Reinforcements trickled in when new recruits came and when they could convince current soldiers to stop running away. Pay for their service was slow and non-existent at best, making it difficult to entice new recruits to the cause.

Benjamin Stuart had joined the militia after a British officer killed his brother after an altercation in a local pub, an altercation his brother Martin had tried to avoid. Of course, an investigation was done, with the local magistrate in the British commander's pocket, who ruled it to be self-defense. Martin was buried in a grave behind the old Pentecostal church with a small ceremony of only family and friends.

Molly, his wife of just six years, had begged Benjamin to just leave it alone. She said that God has a way of working things out, and if it were meant that Martins's death was to be avenged, it would be at the hand of God, not a simple farmer. Benjamin tried to take her advice but could not escape the need to take action. It was then that he enlisted, and two days later, he left home.

Thoughts about leaving his family now haunted and distracted him as the crest of the hill neared. Was it his imagination, or did he smell fire and salted pork? Food had been hard to come by in the last few weeks, and it could just be his overly active imagination combined with an empty stomach. Trent, to his right, could smell it too, as could Roscoe, to his left. The seemingly endless mist now cleared as they neared the clearing at the top of the hill.

It was a camp! As they crouched at the clearing, an eerie feeling came over him. Where were all of the soldiers? Why were the fires still burning? Were they out on patrol? Were they watching in wait to ambush them? As they looked at each other, Benjamin decided to take the lead and stood up to move into the camp, motioning for Trent and Roscoe to follow him. Roscoe moved to a tent nearby as Roscoe kept an eye on the wood line behind the camp. The fires, still burning, tin cans with ale and some type of beans were scattered around the fire. They definitely left in a hurry.

Trent and Roscoe now moved back towards Benjamin as the rest of the squad started to move into the abandoned camp. "Make a quick sweep for supplies; be careful, this is too convenient, " Benjamin whispered.

A few boxes of rations, a sparse handful of ammunition, and a half-drunk bottle of ale later, they moved back towards the hill where they entered the camp. "Do you suppose we should wait a spell for them? Should we burn everything?" His men questioned.

There was no time to answer those questions as several musket shots rang out, accompanied by whitish-grey puffs of smoke from the woods behind the camp. Ambushed! The first thoughts were to take cover and return fire. Trent, with a large hole where his brain used to be, didn't have a chance to react. Benjamin realized he was covered in a warm and wet substance as he dived for cover. What was left of Trent's brain had splattered onto his face and neck. The warm, salty, and copper taste from brain matter made him want to puke, but there was no time for that. Thoughts of Molly and the kids entered his mind as he tried to load his musket.

Molly's warm, soft skin and smile always welcomed him home after a long day. The smell of the dinner she made for the family and the joy and laughter of playing with the kids filled his mind as he aimed up the hill to engage the enemy. He pulled the trigger, and the musket ball hit its target in the right temple. Dirt and rock splattered his cheek, and a sharp pain and blood filled his mouth. The shot fired by his enemy had made its target as well.

Benjamin realized he didn't have long, and if he was lucky, he would die before the Redcoats got to him. He rolled over on his side and looked down the hill. He was looking through some kind of hole in a tree or something down at the hill they had climbed an hour earlier. The mist had disappeared and was replaced by steam from his friend's dying or dead bodies covering the hill.

Something odd about the tree stump gave him this view.

He realized in horror that he was looking through Roscoe. Where his chest used to be. What had

caused this? There was no cannon fire, just muskets and swords in this fight......what the hell?

The thoughts of Molly and the kids came rushing back, and the sudden image of a bloody, dying soldier.

...the soldier resembled him! It was his reflection.

His reflection in the blade of a sword! It was too late; they had found him, and he barely had time to scream before the blade found his heart. His last vision was that of a young boy standing over him….not from here. He thought……….the boy looked sad and troubled, and for a brief moment, he was more concerned for the boy than the hot blood gushing from him and the burning sensations in his chest that had been opened by the British blade…… *Ice cream*

"I scream, you scream, we all scream for ice cream!" Ashton loved ice cream, especially vanilla. Homestyle was his favorite. The thick, delicious taste was overwhelming as he sipped the biggest glass he had ever ordered. Thoughts of his girlfriend ran through his mind, and he wondered how her vacation in Missouri was going. He had been invited to go with them, but Dad had said no this time around. He couldn't be mad. Dad let him go last time with the promise that he would behave.

Himself. And he did. He was a perfect gentleman. Of

course, he had to be...Alice's father was just like his dad, which was good.

The pleasant thoughts of Alice were slowly fading away as the taste of his milkshake went from vanilla deliciousness to sour salt metal. In horror, he realized that the bottom of his frozen treat had turned a dark shade of crimson red, the red that looked so good on his favorite superhero, The Flash! There was nothing super about his drink now as he pushed it away. The red was slowly snaking its way through towards the top. Ashton stared in disbelief as the last of the white was swallowed by the red beast that had taken over his drink.

Looking around, he noticed that he was now alone. There were no customers, no staff, and no other tables except for his. The walls, which once displayed pictures of Elvis, Marilyn, The Fab Four, and other famous "oldies, but goodies," as Dad called them, were gone. They were changing somehow, foggy colored kind of. Shadows began to form on them, and new smells began to replace the vanilla, which turned sour. Gunpowder, something was cooking like meat, either human flesh or pork, and the worst smell of all, something dead.

The walls were completely gone now. Elvis, Paul, Ringo, John, and George had left the building and were replaced by the forest. Trees reached high towards a dark ceiling, no lights now, threatening to reach the ends of infinity. "Wow! I sound like Dad when he's teaching science!" That managed to squeak a little giggle out of him before he heard the scream.

Screams of panic and terror were all around. Grunts, heavy breathing, sounds of bones breaking, crying, and pure fear wiped out all pleasant thoughts from before.

Ashton could see soldiers coming out of the darkness. As they got closer, he recognized the uniforms, torn-ragged, put together with what could be found. Minutemen mixed in with fancy, red, and shiny uniforms of British soldiers! Why was he dreaming about the American Revolution, and what did his milkshake have to do with it?

They weren't fighting now, but continued towards him....not him...what they were looking at? They stopped at what was once table 5 at Larry's Ice Cream and stared with the eyes of ghosts at the middle of the table. His milkshake had taken on a new, hideous, menacing form that was now violently bubbling and licking out in hot, deadly tongues like the fires of Mordor did to that kid with the ring. That wasn't the worst of it...something was in the glass with the devil-vanilla shake....moving its way to the top, now just below the surface... He wanted to take the straw and move it, see what it was....it had now broken the surface....he moved in a little closer and stopped.

The boiling had stopped, and the soldiers had left....Ashton was all alone, well, not really alone - if you counted whatever was in his shake. The suspense ended for him as he realized what had been in his milkshake... a scarred, blood-red human eye, now its once blue shade, was mixed with red and something runny, smelly, and yellow. It seemed to stare up toward the ceiling sky as if looking for something. Then the worst thing that could happen did. The eyeball shifted in the once tasty liquid and was now looking at him. It now had a glowing yellow pupil. Ashton screamed like he had never screamed before.

State of dis-union

The country had never been more unrested than in 2015. Poor leadership in Washington, especially on Pennsylvania Avenue, left many Americans distraught, disgusted, and yearning for the patriotic America of old.

America was now the laughing stock of the free world, spending more time apologizing than defending. Its borders were weak, its military cut to the bare minimum, owing more money to China than all the billionaires in the United States.

Gas prices are at an all-time high, with billions of gallons sitting dormant in our strategic reserves while millions of dollars in oil come into US seaports daily from the Middle East.

Our soldiers were murdered at recruiting stations where they were forbidden to defend themselves, shootings at churches, movie theaters, malls, schools, and every place once thought safe filled the news.

The world was spying on us. We are on them. ISIS had replaced the Taliban as a public threat to our way of life. Freedom of speech was all but gone. You didn't have the right to have an opinion if it offended someone.

Police officers were at the top of everyone's hit list, beating out lawyers and politicians. It was seemingly okay to kill a police officer or to murder our servicemen and women at their place of duty. The media ignored these events, only focusing on those that would incite racial tensions.

It was now frowned upon to own a gun unless you were a thug, and then it was okay because society made you that way. It was okay to rob a liquor store if you needed money for medicine, it was okay to sell crack to a child, and it was okay to walk up to a red light and shoot a cop in the head for no reason, as long as you could blame the act on a bad upbringing or you were doing it for your momma.

The press and most of society looked the other way as little at a time. Our rights and history were destroyed, erased, re-written, distorted, or forgotten because someone was offended. Freedom of religion........................GONE!

Freedom of speech....GONE! Civil War history, monuments, books, parks.....GONE! Especially if it concerned the South and the Rebel flag.

Society, fueled by a liberal media and government administration, had become so concerned with feelings that many were more interested in a former Olympic hero, who realized he should have been born a woman, than the murder of our armed forces by its own so-called "American" citizens.

Yes, the once proud United States of America had become what our forefathers had feared the most… a pansy-ass society of offended, handout-hungry zombies that followed the far-left media that told them what to watch, eat, drink, and wear. They told them what movies to watch and who to vote for, and most of all hid the truth about what their country had become. A nightmare that was not about to end anytime soon.

Shrinkies

The monster eyeball milkshake thing was still fresh in his mind as Ashton sat in Dr. John's office just off Rt. 17. Mom was holding his hand as she talked to the nurse. This was just another psychiatry visit in the long line of "who can explain the psycho teenager."

Most shrinkies, as Ashton had started calling them, were perplexed by his vivid hallucinations and attention to detail when describing them. One shrinkie, Dr. Lars, had commented that he almost believed Ashton had been where he described. He spoke with some "historical accuracy" when he told his stories. His description of food, clothing, and weapons was astounding. His description of wounds and dying, though nauseating to his mom, rivaled some tales told by war veterans around counseling groups at the V.A. Doctor Lars lost faith in his ability to help Ashton and recommended someone to take over the case.

His dad's stories of his military escapades didn't even come close, and as an MP, he had some good stories to tell. Ashton had watched his mom's mouth drop to the floor in a combination disgust-shock-gonna puke when he spun his most recent tale of his visit to the malt shop that served free hideous eyeballs to every paying customer.

A light knock at the door signaled the arrival of his latest shrinkie, Dr. Johns, a medium build of a man with dark hair and a pretty awesome beard to match. This shrinkie had been Ashton's fave so far. He was funny, friendly, and seemed to empathize with what was going on. He did not feed into what many before had called delusional episodes but listened to understand and look for a connection between the visions and how Ashton had presented them.

His thoughts were that something was triggering these events; it could be emotional, could be physical, and part of him wasn't ready to rule something out of the ordinary. Whatever the cause, it needed to be figured out.

Boston

Tommy Hallowman had been in the Boston Police Department since 1995. After a thirteen-year stint with the US Army as an MP, he had moved up the ranks to detective and was just a few years from retirement. He was hesitant to move to Massachusetts after the army; after all, Michigan was where he called home. Michigan, with the Wolverines, Spartans, and Tigers, was a big sports fan, but he could not argue with the chance to be a cop in the town where America all started.

Tom had not been much of a history buff until he moved to Boston and fell in love with the history and old buildings that were at the center of the birth of America.

He sometimes wondered what those brave men and

women would think of their "America" now and were torn between the fact that they would be in awe or feel ashamed of what it had become.

Tom started as a patrolman, driving past the square on Congress Street where the Boston Massacre had occurred, the Paul Revere House on North Square, and the Old North Church at 193 Salem Street in the North.

End of Boston, where the phrase "one of by land, two if by sea, signaled Paul Revere before his midnight ride on April 18, 1775. Of course, the events of that night led to the battles of Lexington and Concord just down the road.

Tom, once in a while, on a seldom day off, would go to the site of the Boston Massacre and just sit and imagine the events of those days, how exciting and dangerous things were. He imagined the men and women in their colonial attire, the heels of their shoes clapping on the cobblestone as they walked across the street to the bakery or blacksmith. Maybe to the local pub, he imagined beer, or ale, was pretty tasty back then and didn't have all of the processed ingredients some have today.

Things were also simpler then as well. No cell phones and cars, no social media sites, and cable TV. Back then, you had to talk to each other and interact socially, not text, snapchat, blog, or insta-whatever that the kids were doing now. Back then, there was no dying after being stalked by a predator on Craigslist or someone pretending to be interested in a relationship on Facebook. Sure, there was the occasional murder in Boston circa 1770-1775, but not "social-media" fueled.

Today, as a member of Boston's' finest, you had to worry about responding to an incident and getting ambushed. People nowadays would just walk right up to your car and blow your brains out. He thought of not making it home to his family; this gave him a sense of dread and fear like he had never known before. But even with all of the despair, he had hope for an American comeback, a return to the values of his forefathers and the ones that began a nation right in his town. He often thought of his army days and the soldiers he served with.

Though stationed at many bases over his twelve-year career as a military policeman, his favorite place was the Correctional Brigade he worked at while stationed at Ft. Riley, Kansas. That's where he met and worked with his best friends. Wow, he would think! That was over twenty years ago. They had managed to keep in touch over the years and had met for a reunion a few years ago. There was talk of another get-together soon, but recent thoughts on this had been sidetracked.

As he drove past Starbucks, he resisted the urge to stop and decided to head home and surprise the family with a night out. He slowed for a turning car, not using a Signal, which most drivers seemed to ignore now, and realized he was near Granary Burying Ground. He seemed to recall some famous early Americans were buried there but could not remember who at the moment. That's when it hit him! The square between the eyes! The worst headache he ever had in his life, and with it, the worst daydream he could ever imagine.

Pie and Blood

British soldiers moved in a column of three towards the little bakery built into the side of the small house on Congress Street. The smell of fresh-baked pieces of bread and pies was a treat for those in the area during that time of day, and the smell was especially wonderful for the King's Army, who tended to just take what they wanted without paying for the goods. Some soldiers did pay. Many thought it was a perk to protecting the town from itself and those pesky Sons of Liberty. Of course, it was a well-known fact that most of the town knew the secret identities of the traitors and were protecting them.

Today especially, the smell was overwhelming, and the men stopped to get some ale and maybe some warm bread or pie. There was a pretty good crowd in the streets today, drawn towards the gossip about the latest attack by the Sons on a local home, known to be loyal to George III, and house the local magistrate that had been responsible for some shameful acts against innocent citizens who supposedly tossed fruit at some soldiers passing by.

The soldiers, with a new recruit today, stopped in front of the store and ordered the new soldier to go get some apple pie without rendering proper payment. It was then that they got the word that the Eight Regiment required assistance at the Custom House on King Street, as it appeared that a crowd of hostile citizens were in the street demanding the soldiers "fire and be damned!"

The soldiers arrived at an out-of-control, taunting crowd of men, women, and children. The crowd spat at the soldiers, yelling and screaming, daring them to open fire. It was then that the young man came out of the crowd, moving his mouth to talk, with no words coming out. This young man did not look like a colonial boy; his haircut, clothes, and body language were different. The crowd behind and around him seemed to slow down and fade somewhat into the background as this boy came forward.

Who was this? His shirt was made of a cloth not worn at this time. The strange design and hideousness of the artwork in itself were satanic and hinted at witchcraft and sorcery. The words on it," Fear the Walking Dead," were of a text that was not recognized. As the boy came closer, a man in the crowd also came forward, dressed in uniform and with a pistol drawn. The man was also not of this time and appeared to rush towards the boy. "NO!

Ashton! STOP!" were his words as he rushed to the boy.

Things slowed down, like in one of those movies where the hero is moving so fast that the rest of the world slows down. The citizens were still screaming, but in slow motion, you could see their spittle coming out and their rotten teeth and discolored tongues as they spoke. People were really ugly in slow motion, and nothing moved much at all, except for that boy. As the boy neared the soldiers, the strange man was almost to him, feeling a desperate urge to stop that young man from whatever was about to happen.

As the boy reached the edge of the group of soldiers, a shot rang out, smoke followed by more smoke, another shot and another, as the musket ball hit him right above the left eye. Blood, bone, and brain tissue splattered and dispersed into the crowd. The severed eyeball found the froth of a freshly drank ale as the young man, with only the right side of his head intact, fell to the ground. As the crowd, soldiers, and strange man approached him, they noticed the apple pie splattered on him and at his side.

A gift to the soldiers to appease them and let the crowd have their say. A pie, now mixed with blood, brains, and bone fragments, was left in the street with the dying boy as it began to rain.

The rain took on a steady tap as Tom realized it

wasn't the rain but someone tapping on his window.

"Are you okay, sir? You pulled over suddenly and almost hit that pole. Are you okay?" When the headache hit, Tom had enough consciousness and forethought to get off the road before he hurt someone. Thank goodness for that!

He was okay, his car was okay, and no one was hurt! Except for the pounding in his head. Why did he have that vision? Why was he in it? Who was Ashton, and why did he know his name was Ashton? And most of all…what the hell was up with that pie?

Philly Steak

Javier Perdiz was never one to jump to conclusions. During his army and civilian law enforcement career, he was always the one to think things through, use logic, and not let emotions get in the way. This, however, had him perplexed, stressed, and considering things that were not explainable by anything he had ever experienced. There were no clues, no method of operation, and nothing pointing to any kind of rational explanation. Hell, even Hulk Hogan, the Miz, and John Cena couldn't have pulled this off.

He thought about all the years of investigative training he had, ranging from MPI to CID, from patrolling the downtown streets to becoming Senior Detective for the Philadelphia Police Department. Javier had seen it all, Murder, rape, theft, vandalism, domestic violence, and drunk and disorderly. Recently, things have become stranger than ever. Graves were vandalized, statues defaced, books missing from the local library, and unmovable objects vanishing into thin air.

The statue just off of Hanover Street, weighing at least a few thousand pounds, had vanished. It depicted a man taking a calm ride on a horse. Of course, it was the statue of Paul Revere, of the Midnight Ride fame. This statue had disappeared, and if it were not for the base, one could argue that nothing stood at that spot.

Where the statue used to stand, part of the Paul Revere Mall, was just a concrete base, no debris, nothing. The statue was easily the most photographed and visited statue in Boston. The odds of someone just driving up and taking this historical monument without a clue or observation were not logical. The Freedom Trail was very well-traveled, whether, by locals or tourists, this was just not possible. No witnesses no clues equals a dead-end report. Javier took one more look around and decided to head back to the precinct to file one of the strangest reports of his life.

Cold coffee! He should be used to it by now. It's what usually happened when he hit the coffee stand and then got a call immediately. He didn't realize he had been on the last call for over two hours. Maybe this loss of time came with age, who knows. He took a sip of the coffee as the next call came in. A theft at the Liberty Bell Center on Market Street. He assumed it was a purse, or someone left a gift from the gift shop lying on a bench, and an opportunistic thief took advantage of it, but that was not the case.

Item stolen, in broad daylight, without any clues or witnesses….in one of the biggest tourist attractions in Philadelphia….the Liberty Bell. As he made his way through the police and media now huddling in a shark feeding frenzy outside of the Liberty Bell Center, he felt it, the slow rumble beneath the concrete, far below the earth. This, accompanied by the biggest migraine he had ever experienced…had to find a seat, a bench, something before he took a tumble.

Just a swingin'

The morning air was cool as the voices approached the edge of the woods. The voices, filled with excitement, entered the clearing and stopped short of a noose hanging above an ale barrel. There were six men, soldiers in red hats with what looked like feathers. No, some kind of decoration, maybe not feathers. They surrounded a single man, bound in rope and looking like he had been through a hellish experience and was now paying for his actions. The soldiers stopped and asked the prisoner to climb up on the barrel, which he did freely, placing the noose around his neck; they asked if he had any last words.

The man mentioned something about only having one life to give for his country, followed by laughter from his executioners, then the kicking of the barrel out from under his feet. The man kicked involuntarily as his eyes bulged, and he gasped for air as he strangled to death at the end of the rope. It was over in a few minutes. What had this man done to deserve this? Javier realized that he was there. He was at this execution. He could smell the death. He could feel the breeze. Why was this?

These thoughts faded as he now realized that British soldiers and the hanged man, Nathan Hale, were here before him, in his dream, right? Was it a bad dream? It had to be! But it felt so real. Maybe if he closed his eyes, he would wake up, maybe laying on the ground at the Liberty Bell

Center, maybe in the hospital. He realized he was hiding behind a tree, which was the key phrase because the soldiers had found him. They were looking and walking his way, weapons drawn.

Should he run, or should he just give up? They were upon him, and he stood up to make it easier for them. As they reached for him, he put his hands out, and they reached behind him, taking the boy from behind him into custody. Where did he come from? He had no idea the boy was there! The boy was not from this time period. He was a young man dressed like kids in Philly: jeans, t-shirt, and sneakers. The kid was wearing a zombie t-shirt and a ball cap, New England Patriots. The soldiers tied his hands with rope and led him away. The boy looked back at him and then pointed to the hanged man.

The hanged man, Nathan Hale, he remembered the school teacher turned patriot from his school days and the History Channel, had now taken on a different persona. His hair and build had changed, his clothes were more modern, he was clean-shaven with no facial hair, and his skin had turned a darker, more Hispanic shade.

The dream had become a nightmarish freak-fest with history taking on a new, personal twist. The executed man's eyes, dead and glassy, were that of Javier Perdiz of the Philadelphia Police Department. The boy had pointed out the truth of the dream. He was a witness to his own execution.

The woods dissolved into lights and sirens. He felt something on his face; the soldiers were trying to suffocate him, and he struggled but realized several hands were holding him down, trying to keep him from getting a breath. "Detective! Calm down. We are trying to help you!" The familiar voice made him open his eyes. He was lying on the floor of the Liberty Center, surrounded by colleagues and paramedics. He was alive, back home. Maybe he never left. Why did he have that dream? Who was the boy? Why did the ground shake when he got the headache? Javier tried to relax as the emergency team put him into ambulance 51.

The Senator

The Senator from the great Commonwealth of Kentucky had just introduced Senate Bill #04181775, to a heavily Democratic Senate. The bill is to confirm the US Constitution, Declaration of Independence, and other historic documents and keep them from being changed, dissolved, or otherwise changed to meet the desires of a nation zombified by the left-wing media. He knew the outcome. Whiny-pansy ass, grease-me-up politicians that had forgotten what they took an oath to do, protect the Constitution and protect America from all threats domestic and foreign fools reacted with negative responses. The sad part is that most threats nowadays were domestic, many probably influenced, even funded by its representatives.

He knew he was in for a tough battle. He did not have the support nor the people on his side. America had become the land of the free…Free handouts, that is.

People were more concerned about what their Uncle could give them than what they could do for America. Damn shame, the great men and women who dared to defy the mighty British government would be ashamed if they could see the American dream become the American Entitlement dream.

He wondered if it was worth the effort as he walked through the underground tunnel that connected the US

Capitol with the "other" underground entrances throughout DC. Could one man or a few make a difference?

He thought about what his good friend Gary had told him. As long as you have a breath, you have some hope.

Gary was a smart man, an actor by choice, a defender of US Veterans rights and one hell of a singer as well. He had made some great movies but was more inspirational with his band and his activities working with our veterans. Gary would make a great leader, maybe even President, but that was not him. He did not want the glory, except for the brave men and women who deserved it. Our country needed more men like Gary. This thought gave him some hope as he entered the elevator that would take him to his office.

One is a lonely number

He was not alone. During his drug-induced sleep, Ashton had found some new friends, ones who seemed like good guys who would protect him. They saw him in the dreams, and he knew they did because they looked right at him and saw him! Was supposed to show them something? He tried to hand the British soldiers some pie, and tried to show one of his new friends that anyone could die for their country, but did they understand?

Mom was shaking his shoulder, trying to wake him. How long had he been asleep? Did they know he was dreaming? He wondered if he should share his latest dreams with Dr. Johns and his parents. He decided to wait and see if he would get to go home. He definitely was not going to share about his new friends, at least until he knew who they were, but most surely he was not going to tell about the dark room with the men meeting in secret, discussing the plans to bring our country to its knees and change it forever. Evil men, with no love of America, no care for its citizens, and most of all, no care how many died in the process. The scary thing was he recognized some of the men from TV.

"Let's go home Ashton!"

Dr. Johns had signed the papers letting him go home, with restrictions, of course. As he watched Ashton get in the car with his parents, Johns wondered if he could even help the boy. What if he could not? Surely, something was triggering these events. He fumbled for his loose change for a coffee between patients. No lunch break today, full schedule. He didn't really like the coffee in the machine, he enjoyed the poker cards on each cup. Fifty cents is a cheap bet, and he really didn't have time for anything else.

The cup ker-plunked into the bottom of the machine and started to fill with hot liquid. He dreaded the taste, but had become somewhat addicted to its bitterness and psychological effect on him. An ace, two fives, a six, and a jack. Loser! Oh well, turning to head back to his office, to catch five minutes of Sports Center before his next patient, he gingerly took a sip of the "Satan's caffeine" as he called it.

SFFFFTTTTT! The liquid left his mouth faster than it had entered it. The liquid had a coppery rubber taste to it and a vile texture that spewed from his lips as soon as he touched it with his tongue. The cup and its contents were now on the floor, the wall, and his smock.

The liquid was darker than an abyss; bubbles in it moved back and forth like it was boiling in the pot. It seemed to have a life of its own, of course he knew this was impossible, or was it? As he moved past the puddle of "death" to get the mop, he slipped on the edge of the mess and down he went. His head hit before anything else, causing a loud rock hitting a concrete block sound.

The last thing he remembered was the ringing in his head and the hot blood pouring from his skull. It was suddenly cold in the hallway, and the steam from his fresh blood rose above him to form an eerie mist……….

The Hills

They were relentless; just kept coming, up the hill, retreat, up the hill again. Waves of them, many would fall, some would keep going. The small group of colonists could not hold them off forever; ammunition was low, and they were so badly outnumbered. This was just the soldiers that had made land from the boats, and the boats were going back for more.

William Prescott's forces had waited for the British to arrive and had formulated a good battle strategy, except they were very short of ammo. The British forces, coming ashore in Boston Harbor, would make it a fair distance up the hill because Prescott's orders were not to "fire until you see the whites of their eyes" to save ammunition. The battle raged for hours, and many a British soldier fell, but alas, you can't fire your musket without ammo.

Doctor Bill Johns was an avid history buff, and often watched the History Channel or thought about his favorite time in history, but this was different. This dream felt so real. He was there, at the top of Breeds Hill, with a musket, fighting beside a child no older than 15 or 16, maybe. This child was a tenacious soldier, screaming as he fired, reloading, waiting for the perfect shot, and firing again.

He looked around at the other Colonial soldiers. They were fighting as hard as they could, but you could see the reality setting in, the ammo was running out, and the British kept comin' but there weren't as many as there were a while ago. Bill smiled. He loved that song by Johnny Horton. Even though he knew that song was about the War of 1812, it seemed to fit this situation.

"This is the Battle of Bunker Hill." Bill knew it well. The song was still stuck in his head as the cannons started firing from the shoreline. Some men started calling for a retreat, but Bill and his young partner stayed the course.

That last cannon blast was close. The tree to the right of them was shattered and smoked from the heat of the shell.

Maybe retreat was a good idea. Bill tried to remember how this battle ended; he knew the Colonists lost and most survived because they ran for their lives when the ammo ran out. Good idea, he thought. He turned to grab his new battle buddy to drag him to safety. It was too late; the young man was dead. He looked down the hill, it was a sea of red, not from blood, but from the red uniforms of the hundreds of British soldiers they had killed, about 600 if he remembered his history right. Steam came up from the bodies, some hours old and already attracting flies. He looked back at the young soldier to his left, the left side of his body shredded by a cannonball; it struck him how much it looked like his star patient, Ashton. The roar of the cannonballs and the resulting impact continued to deluge the hill. It was then that the cannonball replaced the space where his head had been and took his life.

Shake, Rattle, and Roll

It was the biggest earthquake to hit the east coast of the U.S. in forever. The tremors were felt from Savannah, GA, to Boston, MA. There were no warnings. It came and left, ten to twenty seconds at the most, not big on the Richter scale, but widespread. Damage was minor for the most part. There were some areas, small and isolated, that had more damage, mainly cemeteries and memorial gardens, which were hit the hardest. CNN, MSNBC, and Fox News had called it the Quake that didn't shake.

Cemeteries up and down the East Coast were the

recipients of the most damage, an odd fact to most. Mostly tree and fence damage, along with some cracked, crumbled, and knocked-over tombstones. Nancy McCracken was visiting her husband in the corner of section 6 in the Granary Cemetery when the quake hit. She had just told her husband she was going to marry his best friend, and the timing of the quake was quite ironic.

Nancy looked around, right hand with a death grip on the left corner of Homer McCracken's headstone, as she looked around, waiting for the quake to stop. She watched as some older trees fell onto some fence in bad need of repair, as some older stones crumbled, many just falling over in place, and some older graves shifting underground, bringing old coffins to the surface. Strange thing was, as the quake progressed, Nancy felt less and less afraid. She thought of Homer, how brave he always acted and how he would stand defiantly waiting for the "little" rumble from the ground to stop.

The whole event lasted about ten seconds and once Nancy got her sense of balance back, she stood up to survey the damage. Homer's grave, and that of other veterans near him, had no damage. The graves to the left and right had more damage. As Nancy got up and walked towards the "more famous" graves in Granary, she noticed heavy damage. Some graves were destroyed, some coffins, lids shattered, bones and skulls laying in the sunshine, grinning smiles at what had just happened.

Nancy, not the sharpest lady around, noticed that the older the grave, and the bigger the celebrity status of the occupant, the more damage there was. She started to notice this despite her 8th-grade education, and beginnings of Alzheimer's. The last grave in the row made her stop in her tracks. This grave was completely open, and as she stepped up to look, she realized it was empty. The odd thing was who the grave belonged to.

Zombies

Reports from other cemeteries, up and down the East Coast were the same, with minor damage for the most part, except for certain parts of the site. Minor damage to extreme damage, the more famous the grave, the more the damage. Tom just got done his morning patrol brief and was going to get him a nice cup of Joe, when the call came in to check out quake damage at Granary.

The quake, only a few hours past, had only done minor damage, with fewer than expected damage and 9-1-1 calls. Nancy, a local regular contacting the police, had called it in, telling her story about Homer and the missing bodies that were probably walking around, signaling the arrival of the zombie "poco-lips," as she called it. Tom really hoped she had left the scene.

Granary Burial Ground was the final resting place of many a soul, a lot of them from the American Revolutionary period. Many veterans, former city leaders, and founding

Bostonians lay there. It was one of many hot-spot in the city where America was born. As Tom drove down Congress Street for the hundredth time, he noticed little damage to anything. How the hell was this a 5.5? What would we do with a 7.5? Tom had left home this morning, ready for anything, looking forward to the three-day weekend coming up. Three-day weekends were hard to come by, and a day off was hard to come by recently.

His prayers had come true; Nancy was nowhere in sight. Maybe she had gone home, thank god, he did not need to see her today. The patrols that initially responded to the scene had blocked off the road and fifty feet in front of the scene. The local media, looking for anything negative, as usual, had beaten him to the scene. Tom grabbed his ID and made sure he had his gun as he exited his 1973 Ford Falcon Coupe, yes, of the Mad Max fame, and headed towards the officers securing the entrance.

"What's up, Max?" They kidded him; secretly jealous of Tom's awesome car. His wife called it his midlife crisis and he didn't care; the car was awesome and most of all, it was his. There was more damage on the inside of the cemetery than outside. Weird, he thought, but blamed it on coincidence. There were a few officers standing near some of the more extensive damage, and some taking pictures. "It's the start of the Zombie Horde, I tell you!" It was Nancy, still hanging around, dammit he thought to himself. Maybe they already took the loony broads statement, and then I won't need to talk to her.

Tom noticed Julia waving him towards the back of the cemetery, a spot reserved for all the famous residents of Granary. "Got a weird one here, Tom. Someone stole some bodies after the quake." She paused, and then continued; "now the super-weird, some of the bodies were a few hundred years old, and couldn't have been much more than dust and rags." Tom pondered that for a second and then spoke. "OK, anything else?" He was surprised at the answer he got. "Sir, one was Sam Adams."

Tom turned to walk away, the only thing he could think of was "Damn, I love his beer." It was going to be a long, strange, and coffee-filled day, followed by an evening of many beers.

Fair and Balanced

Ashton and his dad were watching the quake news on Fox News Channel, discussing the science behind quakes, when Ashton asked why his dad watched Fox News. "Because it's fair and balanced news reporting!" was his response. They looked at each other and laughed. Dad was a diehard, old man republican, according to his sons, and was the butt of many of their liberal jokes as he called them. They both knew that there was no news channel that was fair. There were all of those who supported the current administration, and then there was Fox News.

"Dad, we need to talk, there is something going on."

Dad, a director of a local childcare facility, knew when to listen, and now was a time to listen. Ashton told him of his most recent dreams, about the people he saw, the events that took place, and the fact that he saw people from today that he somehow knew were real, not from the past. "These guys saw me as well, so I know they had the same dream as me! That's not all," he continued, "I had one more dream, and I think this one would be easy to check up on." The dream lived again as Ashton looked his father in the eyes and began.......

His dream started with music, the Dropkick Murphy's song, the one on the beer commercial was playing as he walked through an iron fence into a graveyard. There were graves everywhere, none of them of any significance except for the one in the back. Some type of light was shown on it. It was weird because it was nighttime, and there was no moon, no street lights, nothing that could have illuminated that grave. A foggy, backlight type of mist rose from the grave, which he realized was open, with no dirt pile like you usually see near an open grave; the light-fog-mist cloud swirled around in and out of the grave, and Ashton was a little scared to move closer. He mustered up some courage and moved closer....

The dirt was gone from the grave, the lid was gone from the coffin, and it appeared empty. Initially, he thought to turn around and go home, but he could not do so. Something was making him look again. But he didn't want to look; he was afraid the grave would not be empty now. OK, one more time, and then I'm leaving. The craziest thing was that Ashton knew he was dreaming. He could not help himself. He knew he would not wake up and he had to look.

This time there was movement in the shadows, a shifting of weight, something moving against dirt and wood. It was weird because it did not sound like a body but a stick or bone moving around in a wood box. He peered into the darkness a little more, wondering why his dreams never included flashlights or M-16's, or bazookas, or pirate swords, or anything that actually helped. He could feel movement, air in his face, a breath maybe? Just the wind picking up? It got closer, stronger, now with a stench, death? Decay? It reminded him of Dad's breath after some beers and some sausage pizza. He dream-giggled, and for a moment, his fear was gone. Dad sure loved his beer and pizza! He wished Dad was in his dream, but like he said, his dreams never tossed in anything that would help him.

The breeze had stopped, the stench was still there, and another feeling, the light touch feeling you get when an ant is crawling on your arm, so light, but you can tell it was there. He went to pull his arm back, but something had grabbed his wrist and was pulling him into the darkness. He felt like a slow-motion movie; he could feel forward movement, but it took forever, with light now showing in the darkness.

The light, at first dim, now got brighter and took on a

more defined shape. Round eye-shaped lights were now in front of him, and he realized it was something dead pulling him into the grave. It was pulling him down into the abyss of death for him to start a new life with a dead guy, a strange Tales from the Crypt kind of moment. The last thing he remembered was the eyes blinking and a whisper in his ear.

Dad had sat mesmerized, maybe even a little scared, as Ashton relayed that last dream. "But Dad, the weirdest thing happened after the dream." He was reaching in his pocket now. "I had this when I woke up." His wrist, bruised with fingerprint-hand shapes twisting a swollen bracelet mark all the way around it, and in his hand was a crumpled piece of paper. Written on the paper, in an old text, were the words: "We the people." That was it. He knew what it was from, but not sure what it meant. "Where was this cemetery? Do you know?" He looked to Ashton for an answer. "It was Boston, Dad. It was the grave of Samuel Adams. Do we tell mom?"

Dad decided now was not the time.

Philadelphia

Philadelphia experienced the quake as well, minor damage in most places, a little extreme in some, and most of it at the cemeteries around the city and suburbs. Same thing, some bodies missing, only it was a little weirder. Javier Perdiz had spent his morning trying to motivate himself to go to work again. He loved his job, but the recent atmosphere hanging over the city of "Brotherly Love" had been crazy. Murder rates were up, robberies up, and assaults were at an all-time high. He was earning his money this week.

Javier headed to Christ Church to check out the report there. Christ burial grounds were a pretty full cemetery with around 1400-1500 graves marked there, many more graves than that, with most likely 5,000 more grave markers missing from erosion over the past couple of hundred years. Many famous people are buried there including five signers of the Declaration of Independence. The Church on 2nd Street was built in 1695 and was a popular stop for tourists and school field trips.

Javier arrived at the same hoopla that his old army buddy, Tom, did in Boston. Patrolmen securing the gate, the local news media just waiting to get in, and a crowd of gawkers with nothing else to do but blocking the street to see what was going on or get on the local news at six or ten. Javier spoke to the rookie cops guarding the entrance, highly advising them not to let the press in, and headed to the center of the graveyard, where he knew Sgt. Klous would be. Sgt. Klous, one of the many army veterans on the PPD had been on the force almost as long as Javier, but had not moved up the ranks as fast, but chose to remain a patrolman rather than move up to detective.

Javier found the Sgt. just where he thought he would be. He was standing in front of a grave that looked like a tornado, flash flood, earthquake, and a six-alarm fire had been through. The grave was wide open, the ground flooded with what looked like a rain storm had been through, the tombstone smashed, and the coffin looked like it had spontaneously combusted. Half in and half out of the coffin was a badly burned body, hands clenched as if it felt the burning of the fire, its clothes melted to its body and the smell of burning flesh was overwhelming.

"So Brian, what do you think happened?" Javier questioned him.

"I thought we had a missing body." Sgt. Klous paused before he answered to either collect his thoughts or to not sound like a smart-ass to his superior and then spoke.

"Well, sir, we do have a missing body.

First of all, this is not the fellow from the grave." He noticed Javier's puzzled look and continued.

"This poor bastard here had flesh to burn; he felt the pain of whatever happened to him because his hands are in a wretched position, and he's wearing Wal-Mart jeans." He continued, "The body in the grave was in there for over two hundred years, and I doubt it would have survived a fire." Javier moved to the body and realized the Sgt. was right. This had been a man, probably in his 30s, decent health, and had a tattoo of a skull on his left shoulder. So, where was the body from this grave? He looked up as a forensics tech was raising up the collapsed tombstone, the name on it……Benjamin Franklin.

Javier remembered his experience earlier at the Liberty Bell Center, and wondered if the two connected somehow. Looking around for evidence, he remembered the boy he saw in the vision of his execution, and wondered how he tied into this? He remembered the news earlier that other major cities up and down the east coast had experienced some of the same issues and decided it was time to call Tom.

Kentucky calling

Ashton fell asleep playing GTA V, his favorite game. Dad thought it was okay. After watching him play a few times, but always reminded him that it was just a game "cause that's what fathers do." With Ashton asleep, he decided to call his old army buddy in Boston to see if he could shed any light on what was going on.

"Tom, old friend, how's it going in Beantown, being a Tiger fan and all?" The two had not spoken on the phone in a few years, just kept in touch on Facebook, so it was a tiny-bit awkward. After asking about each other's family and the usual pleasantries, he got to the real reason he called. After explaining Ashton's dreams, their location, and tossing in a few other things only a dad could pick up on, he waited for Tom's take on everything.

"Well, Larry, things here are pretty strange as well.

The statue of Paul Revere is gone, the corpse of Sam Adams went on a walk-about, and some other old bastard skeletons are missing as well. We have all officers looking into some pretty strange stuff. I talked to Javier, and things in Philly are pretty screwed up as well. The cemeteries are pretty messed up and they have some missing corpses as well. Ben Franklin is gone and I suspect he may have met up with Sam Adams to slam down a few Boston Lager's. Get this though, at Granary, where Sam Adams should have been, was a crispy fried body, not Sam though because this one was only about thirty or so."

Tom went on, "also, Javy went to check on another missing item, not a corpse though…..the Liberty Bell just vanished, but that's not the strange part. It went bye-bye in between tours, with a building full of people. I have other friends in Yorktown, D.C. and New York who have some wild events as well. So it's not isolated." Larry took it all in before he decided to tell Tom the one thing he had left out.

"Tom, there's one other thing. Ashton tells me he had a dream about the Boston Massacre, he was killed in it, he also mentioned apple pie and the fact that you were there. He described you perfectly." Dead silence followed that last comment for what seemed like an eternity. It was a dead, we are all going to die type of silence. Tom cleared his throat, almost sounding like a muffled cry of terror was trying to escape a suddenly dry throat.

"Larry, Javy saw something as well. There was a young boy very out of place. He was in my dream as well. I think it was your son."

Before hanging up, they agreed to a conference call with Javy later in the week after they did some more research. For now, Larry would question Ashton for more details without alarming him, or his mother. The best thing to do now was to keep a clear head, maybe talk to Dr. Johns to see what he thought. As he was picking up the phone to make that call, it rang, almost causing Larry to drop the phone, it was Dr. Johns, and he didn't sound very good.

New York

New York was less affected by the rolling quake than most of the east coast. Some of the outlying, less concrete areas had more damage, but not much. The cemetery hit the hardest was at Trinity Church. Trinity Church had several different grave areas, and they were all hit about the same. The quake crumbled, collapsed, and relocated tombstones, coffins up out of the earth and some corpses missing. Just like Philadelphia and Boston, the body of a notable forefather was missing.

JoAnn Butler was visiting the grave of her uncle while in New York visiting her friend Maria. Maria had to work that day so JoAnn took a taxi to Trinity Church to visit her uncle Bob. Though she never really knew him, she had heard a lot about the cemetery and really wanted to visit. Today was a beautiful morning, sunshine with a cool breeze; birds singing, flowers blooming, a beautiful New York day.

When the quake hit, she did not know what it was. Being from Kentucky and all, this was out of the ordinary.

The first thing she did was find a tree to wrap her arms around until the ground stopped shaking. The whole thing seemed to last forever. Tree limbs were falling, headstones falling over, crumbling, and just plain exploding out of the ground. Looking to her left, she saw the corner of a casket spike through the ground into the sunshine, with many others following. She thought of her family, back in Kentucky and wondered if this was happening there as well. Silly girl, she thought, that is seven hundred miles away; of course, it's not happening there.

She thought of Ashton and all the problems he was having. Poor kid, no one deserves those horrible nightmares. He was a good kid, had a nice girlfriend, awesome grades, never into drugs, or had run-ins with the police. She needed to get home to her family. As soon as this was over, of course; it seemed to last forever, but in reality, she knew it only lasted a matter of seconds.

At last, it had ended, and everything seemed to calm down, except for one area of the cemetery; there was some smoke or dirt being tossed around and she could not help but go look. JoAnn slowly moved towards the area that had not calmed down and noticed that this grave was destroyed, coffin out of the ground, shattered, and the worst thing off all, she did not see a body.

Curiosity killed the cat – and she was very curious to know whose grave this was. As she approached the headstone, she noticed it was covered with blood, and looked as if it was shot with something, a pistol, maybe? Her husband had been in the army, but was not a big gun guy.

She moved closer to the old tombstone and realized this person had lived a few hundred years ago. Some of the letters were hard to read, she could make out "lex" and "ham" with no problem. The rest was hard to read. She moved closer....a little closer and could now read "Alex" and "Hami." Alex Hami? OK, that was a weird name. She reached out to touch the stone, and as her fingers made contact, the ground began to rumble, and the earthen grave swallowed her.

Cpl. Jenks knew this cemetery well. It was part of his usual patrol, and he could tell you who was here, how long, and what brought them here. His favorites were the ones that were not so famous. He liked to come here on his lunch break and Google the names he was not familiar with and see if he could find out more about them. He then kept a notebook of what he learned. Maybe a strange hobby to some, but he knew more about the residents than most tour guides did.

Today was different at Trinity. The ground had mysteriously spewed out some coffins. The shaking had destroyed some markers, and for a few seconds, the usually peaceful setting was one of utter chaos. Jenks moved around to survey the damage and made notes of what he found. He noticed one grave in particular that seemed heavily damaged. This grave needed no Google, no Internet. It was the grave of Alexander Hamilton. He was familiar with Mr. Hamilton, as were most Manhattans. A duel had ended his life long before he could complete his commitment to public service, and he now was the most famous resident of Trinity.

As he approached the grave, he noticed the blood and bullet damage to the headstone. That's weird, he thought, never noticed that before. He looked into the grave, thinking he would get a glimpse of the dusty bones of one of the most famous Americans to ever live. It did not happen. The grave was empty? Or was it empty?

There was a small purse on the ground nearby, and a cell phone. That didn't come out of the grave. Upon looking further, he noticed a foot sticking out from under the coffin. There's Alexander! No, wait, this foot had flesh, it was a woman's foot, and it moved its toes just a little. Cpl. Jenks called 9-1-1 as he was hopping into the grave to rescue whoever had fallen into this predicament.

Zombies, Wildcats, and maggots...

Oh my!

Andy was just finishing his first semester at the University of Kentucky; it had been as easy as he thought it would be. There was no home sickness, only missing his parents a little, no problems at all. His grades were great, he had made new friends, and all of his professors and advisors loved him. He was well on his way to his career goals, a lawyer-psychologist-CSI kind of career. He could not wait. He enjoyed the visits from mom and dad once a month and he was expecting them this coming weekend. If mom returned from New York, Dad and Ashton could get Dr. Johns to allow Ashton to travel.

He had been worried about his younger brother for the last few months; his dreams had gotten worse, and there had been more trips to the hospital. Andy had experienced a few bad dreams, but nothing he could not handle. It was a wonderful Saturday morning as he headed to breakfast to meet some friends from high school. The four of them had come to UK together, but because of different career paths, they did not have any classes together. This was going to be a good day.

Catching up was awesome. It was great to see his friends. But Andy felt something was not right. He was usually pretty right on when these feelings came. His friends noticed his lack of "fun" and finally got him to tell them of his feeling of impending doom. When he got back to Champions Court, he decided he would call home tomorrow. He lay down to sleep.

The branches broke under his feet as he ran for his life. He kept looking back, expecting to see whatever it was that was chasing him. For some reason, he could not remember why he was running. Andy did not recognize the woods he was running through; they did look familiar, but right now was not the time to think, it was time to run like hell. The trees went by like blurs of cars moving along the interstate. He could make out people sitting on benches, walking their dogs, playing Frisbee, and having a picnic under the tree. They didn't seem to see him though and that made him stop in his tracks.

He went to see his friends, and then it was back to his room. He was dreaming and any minute now he would wake up. He was sure of it. He looked around. He had to be invisible. The cute girl that just ran by him, didn't even smile. The dog to his right wasn't barking.

The runner that just side-swiped him didn't say a word, not even a WTF. What was going on here? He observed some movement to his left from around the running path, behind the group of trees that he did not see earlier.

There were some men walking towards him now, something odd about them though. They moved very slowly, with little energy, and with seemingly no reason or purpose at all. Their faces were gray and the features were blurred and seemed like ash and mold. Who are these guys, and why won't I wake up? As they came closer, he knew he needed to run again, but he could not. He had to see who these guys were.

They were dressed funny, like those actors you see dressed up to pretend they were living in the past.

Maybe Civil War dudes, maybe earlier, anyway, they were a mere stone toss away from him now. They did not speak; the smell of them got his attention, the smell of rotten meat, the kind that attracts wiggly, gross maggots to the trash can when you toss raw meat into it a few days before the garbage man comes.

He thought he might see some maggots, but did not. Time to run; they were right on top of him now. He knew it was his imagination. This could not be happening. It was those Buffalo wings he ate last night! That had to be it. He went to bed, and got an upset stomach, which was causing a nightmare. He turned to run, just as one of them grabbed his shoulder, one grabbed his waist, and the other one grabbed his feet. He was getting away, no… he was not! He felt cold, wet, bony hands pulling him to the ground.

Why wasn't anyone helping him? The park was full of people! What the hell, hey you bastards, he thought, why aren't you helping me? He was on the ground now and the "things" were rolling him over to finish him off, eat him, or something. Maybe it wasn't a dream, but a prank perpetrated by his friends to punk him.

If that was the case, they had gone too far! The monster at the leg was now taking a bite out of him, as was the one at his shoulder. The other one was now close enough to his face to actually be seen. Andy stared in horror into a face he recognized all too well- a face most Americans would know. As he tried to escape this nightmarish American Horror Story of a dream, he could only think one thing: his family, and the hopes that he would wake up soon. He writhed in pain, disbelief, and sheer terror as Benjamin Franklin sunk his rotting, maggot-infested teeth into his neck. He could feel the slimy, wiggly maggots crawling on his neck with his final thought….God bless America…

Went to a garden party

The news finally had a report of the strange occurrences around the nation, not the quakes, and how it affected transportation etc., but the missing bodies, attacks on random people, and the items of historical value that were missing. The far left media, which for the last 8 years, had been dancing on the lap of Washington, D.C. and its millionaires, was now reporting something that was not puppeteered by the White House, nor did it have anything to do with racism, someone being offended by something stupid, or police bashing.

They were reporting the mysterious happenings surrounding the nation's monuments, memorials, and its history; a history that many self-centered-what can you give me citizens had been told to forget by the media and politicians. It was on every channel now, replacing the story of the school system in Tennessee that would not allow its students to wear the American flag on clothing, or as a patch, or in any form whatsoever; replacing the story of the American Hero/athlete that decided he wanted to be a woman; replacing the whining about being offended, and most of all…. Replacing the race for the White House that offered no real alternative for the hot mess, freak on a leash administration that had led (used loosely) the country for so long.

Larry, Javy, and Tom had left their jobs to meet for the

first time in years. Larry had also called Cpl. Jeff Jenks to join them at a local tavern just outside of Ft. Riley, Kansas; Jeff could not make it, but was available for a conference call if needed. It was a Friday afternoon and Larry had already polished off a few beers before Tom and Javy arrived. Larry remembered the bar, they used to come here all the time when they had the apartment up the road. Good times, a bit simpler back then. Didn't have kids to worry about, bills were limited then too, and they had no cell phones or the Internet then either.

Javy, and Tom were present by seven pm and Larry had already had a few more. After hellos and the cordialities were exchanged, they ordered some dinner, followed by a few more beers, then a few more. Finally they were drunk enough to consider what they had come there to think about. The something to think about was going to take alcohol to even consider the possibilities.

Larry started; he talked about all of the issues that Ashton had had recently, what he thought about it, and what he considered the cause to be. Tom and Javy both related stories of what had gone on in their part of the world as well.

Whatever this was; was widespread and weird as hell. Weirder than being at guest at Oprah's for dinner was the example he used. As they contemplated what to do they saw more craziness on the evening news. KSNT was broadcasting from various locations up and down the east coast. Reports of more graves and missing old guys like John

Hancock and Crispus Attucks from Granary in Boston; Thomas Jefferson, gone missing from Monticello, James Madison from Montpelier, Horatio Gates from Trinity, and even George Washington got up from his grave at Mount Vernon to go on a most excellent adventure. There was definitely something afoot at the Circle K, most assuredly.

The discussion then went to the old days, before today's army became whipped and afraid of its own shadow, before don't ask, don't tell, and before the flag of the United States of America started to offend its own populace, now over run by touchy-feely entitlement whores that were dragging the country down.

They all agreed that it wasn't the soldiers fault; they were just led by life-long millionaire senators who only had their own self-interest in mind. There was no Patriotism anymore, no sense of pride, and definitely no sense of the responsibility that once had America as world leader, not world apologizer.

By the end of the evening, ok, early morning, they decided to keep in touch by calling or texting what they had learned every day. They would all go back and investigate, keep notes, and come up with the next step in the plan, as soon as they figured out what was going on. As Larry was leaving, he received a call from the local hospital in New York, his wife had been hurt. He called Ashton, who was spending the night with a friend, and informed him that he would have to detour to New York before returning home.

As he hung up and reached for his keys to the rental car, the phone rang yet again. Dr. Johns was very excited as he told his story…..

New York

The plane ride to New York took forever and by the time Larry got to the hospital, Jo Ann, his wife, was being released to go home. He gave her a hug and kisses as he listened to the doctor explain how they found her under a casket and she was lucky she did not suffocate under the dirt and the weight of the old wood. As they rode back to the airport he told her everything that was going on, leaving nothing out. Now was not the time to worry about her feelings or scaring her. Now was the time to find out what was going on, and it centered on Ashton.

Jo Ann told her amazing story of the earthquake, falling into the hole, and of the brave officer that had rescued her. Larry was astonished that her rescuer had been Jeff, whom he had just spoken to over the phone earlier. Why didn't he mention this? Wasn't it important? Maybe he didn't put the facts together? Larry remembers the call with Dr. Johns and decided to tell his wife about it, regardless of the outcome. As he watched the expressions on her face change like the Cleveland Browns change quarterbacks, he held her hand, and assured her they would figure it out together.

Washington

The District was abuzz with a news report about a young man that was having visions about the wild events happening all up and down the east coast. Though no names had been released, they knew it was someone from the Commonwealth of Kentucky. A special subcommittee, meeting in secret, had briefed the President on the strange occurrences and the young man that seemed to have something to do with it. Of course, the administration knew who the boy was, but if it got leaked to the press, every paper, TV station, and magazine in the world would be after the story before they had a chance to interview him.

It was crucial to get to him first, quell any possible news stories that could hurt the administration, and to find out what was going on. If needed, they would detain, (arrest) the family, of course for their protection and national security reasons. The President was worried about her legacy, after all, she was the first woman president and had to cement her place in history. The last thing she needed was to give the other party ammunition in the next election.

The ground rumbled again as the president moved to the secret room she had come to love hiding out in. She had plenty to be ashamed of now days. All of her promises had fallen through, her cabinet devastated by scandal, lies, and rumors; well for the most part. She had problems of her own as well. This was a tough job to have and she had it tougher because she was a woman.

She blamed her opponents and that News Network that claims to be fair and balanced. The rumble subsided, maybe a four pointer, these came more often in the last few days. Just what she needed, a panicked public, already suspicious, already questioning her administrations every move. She was really going to need a drink tonight.

Bill and Larry

Doctor Johns cut right to the point. He knew Ashton's visions were not nightmares, they had a valid reason for occurring and Larry had to agree with him. Everything tied in together now, the visions, the quakes, the unexplained corpses now seemingly roaming the earth. Not to mention the phone call Larry got from Andy just an hour or so ago. Andy sounded scared and shaken, not usual for the level-headed young man.

It wasn't just Ashton anymore, it was his family and friends, the nation was experiencing something, something that gave him the feeling of doom, despair, and agony on me…… deep, dark depression, excessive misery…….was the song that kept playing through his head every time he tried to rationalize what was going on. They needed a plan of action; they needed to meet, to plan for what might be coming.

Dr. Johns would take a few days off when Larry got his friends and family together; then they would discuss what was going on, entertain ideas, both rational and not; then agree on who would do what. Either way, this was going to be interesting.

Stones and bullets

Allan moved through the alley with his pint of ale towards the voices. He didn't recognize them, but could tell they were agitated about something. As he reached the square he saw a crowd throwing stones at a house and recognized the house as that of Ebenezer, not sure of his last name, but he was loyal to the king. Many citizens did not like him at all. It was then that the thought hit him, maybe he had too much ale, but why was he in Boston, how did he know who Ebenezer was?

He was a long way from Kentucky….wait….a long time from Kentucky. Allan was always one to wait and see what would happen, and since he did not see any way of getting out of the dream, he decided to let it play out.

The crowd continued to throw stones, yell obscenities, and tease Ebenezer. Ebenezer, now visible at the window told them to leave before something bad happened that he would regret. As he watched the crowd he recognized his brother, Ashton? It couldn't be- he was at Joshua's house, wasn't he? Ashton was joining in with the crowd yelling at the occupants of the house, even tossing a stone or two. He tossed his ale to the side and moved towards his brother to see what was going on.

Time seemed to slow at this point and he felt like he was miles from Ashton, instead of feet. Almost there…..he yelled out to Ashton to look his way, but nothing came out, he tried flailing his arms, no response.

As he reached his time travelling sibling, he heard the shots ring out, screaming and running for cover ensued, mass hysteria, the shots were coming from the building under harassment and the occupants had obviously had enough. Now there was screaming, and blood – lots of blood. Ashton was on the ground, several others as well. As he moved to check Ashton, he realized the others were children as well, out a' protesting with their parents tonight. A great family outing!

They all appeared to be dead. He looked back to his brother, whose eyes were wide open, a portion of his chest missing, leaving a hole filled with blood, like a pothole in the middle of I-65 after a rainstorm. It was then that he decided to scream. He wasn't a screamer usually, but today he was. He let out a blood-curdling, Jason-is-back-again type of scream that Jamie Lee Curtis would have been proud of. The sound of the dog barking in step with a loud knocking on the door replaced his scream and he woke up……

A star is born

It was a crisp 57 degrees that morning along 31W. Not much traffic yet, it was only 4:30, the Fort Knox rush of traffic was at least 2 hours away. The identical white SUV's drove north towards their destination. Now just minutes away they hoped to be the first News team on the scene. They needed this story to stay atop the local ratings. The Louisville area had more than its share of local news stations and it was tough to stay on top. Now with the East Coast and the rest of the nation on edge, they could scoop their peers, as well as big dogs CNN, FOX, and MSNBC. Pulitzer prizes, interviews on late night television, their own reality shows – all of this hanging in the balance.

As they pulled into the driveway, they went down the usual checklist....cameras on shoulders- check, microphones ready - check, bright lights to intimidate the family – check, sarcastic- I don't give a damn about your privacy attitudes – check. Everything they needed. They huddled at the front door, ready to pounce on the first person to answer the door......

"Shut up Shadow!" he yelled towards the dog as he rolled off of the couch to see what moron was knocking at oh dark thirty. Reaching for the door, he could hear excited whispering, reminders to shush or they will hear us, and what he thought were little girls giggling like they were playing a prank on someone. As he opened the door, the bright camera light flooded the room like a night train on a dark country stretch of railroad, the fat slimy hand in his face managed to almost choke him with what tasted like a microphone.

"Ashton!" they shouted, "tell us about your dreams! When did they start? Do you see dead people? Have you seen Elvis?" The stupid reporter's questions continued until someone realized that this was not Ashton.

"Hey! You're not Ashton!" Allan finally was able to explain that his younger brother was not home, and after making them believe he did not know where that was, they left.

Allan picked up his cell phone to call dad. He needed to know about this, and the dream he had with his younger brother in attendance.

Let it snow

Alexa lay beside her husband of just a few weeks.

Things had been pretty good for them so far. Other than the usual issues, bills, school, and work, they had a great life. Today had been a tiring day and she was ready for sleep. She snuggled up to Nate as they drifted off to sleep, until the cold came. This wasn't just a somebody-left-the-damn-window open again cold; this was a bone-chilling, ice-box coffin type of cold. The type that you freeze to death and become a human f'ing Popsicle type of cold. The snow pinged against her wind-burned face as the sloshing noise continued. Where was she? What was the sloshing noise? Why wasn't she in her bed anymore?

Where was Nate? Was the bedroom window open? Alexa realized that she was in a boat, and the sloshing was the oars in the water as she and other people moved towards a flickering light in the distance.

There were buildings, more like tents in the distance, smoke billowing up on what was a very cold night. Before she realized it, they had reached the shore and were getting out. The men were soldiers, but not the kind of soldiers she was used to seeing. No camouflage uniforms, no M-16s; they were poorly dressed, including shoes.

Speaking of shoes, she thought to herself, she was barefoot, what kind of dream had you walking through the snow without shoes? She had no coat, only her Batman pajamas. It was bitterly cold, and she desperately wanted to wake up.

That was when all hell broke loose. Gunfire, explosions, and screams filled the night. The soldiers were moving through a small encampment and the occupants didn't even know they were coming. Many men ran out into the cold night trying to put on uniforms and equipment. Alexa realized these were British soldiers from the American Revolution, why? She hated history in school, but she was smart enough to realize this was something she had read about. Some of the men were taking shelter behind what looked like a pile of logs, maybe the beginning of a shelter, and she joined them. Her fingers, nose, and toes were so cold now that she could not feel them, and she swore they weren't even there now.

The weird thing was that none of the soldiers with her acted like she was even there. Not one offered to give her a coat, or a scarf, or something. She reached out to touch the shoulder of one of them….nothing…nothing at all! She closed her eyes and thought of her warm bed, with her warm husband. Maybe she could recite something to wake up. "There's no place like home.

There's no place like home!" Nothing, she begged God to let her wake up, promising to go to church every week, and put more money in the offering plate. Nothing. Some of the soldiers had moved to a small set of trees to the right, only one soldier remained with her.

"It will be all right, Alexa. I promise you." The soldier had spoken to her! She turned around to make sure she wasn't dreaming in her dream and caught a glimpse of the soldier's face in the cold, blustery, moonlit night; the face was very familiar, the boyish grin, and the messed up hair, it was Ashton. Why was her younger brother in her dream? She reached out to touch him, hug him, and hold on until the dream was over. He wrapped his arms around her and tried to comfort her until it was all over. Something was wrong, though, why was Ashton here? Why was he a soldier? Where were they?

She heard a commotion in the distance and some soldiers speaking another language; she recognized it as German, and now the dream was really getting weird. Why were the Americans attacking British and German soldiers? It did not make sense. She turned back to Ashton to seek some answers and realized in horror that something terrible had happened. She reached for him and felt something horribly wet and sharp. As her brother fell into the light of the winter moon, she saw that she had been holding the bloody stump and shattered bone of where his left arm used to be. His eyes were glassy and dead; he had died instantly, maybe from shock, maybe loss of blood. She tried not to cry. It was only a dream, maybe. She put her hand on his face and told him she loved him. The explosion just to her right tossed debris and soldiers everywhere....she was going to die in her dream, she knew it, if only she could wake up.

"Alexa, wake up, you're as cold as ice!"

It was her husband. "Wake up dammit." He wrapped his arms around her and shook her. Finally waking up, she started to cry and buried her head in his shoulder. They just laid there for a few minutes until she was able to calm down and talk. She told him about the dream, and how real it felt. She described in detail how Ashton had been there, and how he had died.

She wanted to call home and check on her brother. It was three thirty in the morning and she knew that all the cell phones would be on vibrate. She talked herself into waiting until morning. "It was only a dream; he is ok, baby." She liked how he could make everything seem ok with just his voice. Something was still not right. Her attention went to the bottom of the bed, her feet were still cold, and there was something else.

Now, they were both looking towards the bottom of the bed as she moved to pull the blanket and sheet off of her feet. The bottom of the bed was soaked, wet with snow and ice; her feet were covered with leaves and dirt, also something else that resembled skin, blood, and flesh! It can't be, she thought, her husband looked on in sheer disbelief as Alexa moved the leaves from in between her toes and wiped the now melting snow off of her pinkish feet. It was real! But how?

Her husband, now a believer, was now pointing to something further down the bed, covered in dirt and blood.... Fabric, maybe wool, soaked in blood. They noticed it was the end of a sleeve, a button at the cuff, looking as if it was ripped from a uniform. Was this the shirt Ashton was wearing? She really needed to call home now. They agreed to go make a pot of coffee and wait until morning to call.

They weren't the only ones awake from Alexa's nightmare. In Kentucky, Ashton woke from a dream about accompanying George Washington across the Delaware River to surprise the Hessians at Trenton. He did not expect to see his sister in his dream. He expected to die mostly because that was how his dreams ended. What he really didn't expect was the snow, ice, and leaves that trailed from where his shoes were at the end of the bed, into the hallway, down the stairs, and out the front door.

More things go missing

There were now hundreds of corpses missing; rumors ran wild about George Washington being spotted at the Opry Hills Mall in Nashville. Tom Jefferson had attended a local art show in Topeka, and Betsy Ross was observed in a Victoria's Secret in Winchester, VA. That wasn't all. John and Samuel Adams were seen in a local Boston tavern, knocking back a few Winter Ales, and Ben Franklin, known to have entertained a few women in his time, was placed at an LA hotspot known for its professional ladies.

Historic documents had been stolen or misplaced, the Declaration of Independence, to name one, the Constitution, Bill of Rights, Articles of Confederation, Emancipation Proclamation, and the Louisiana Purchase; all missing. Of course, usually, when things like this happens, people turn to eBay to get rid of it, or Facebook to brag about it. Social media was quiet. There were no clues.

Also, many statues from historical sites, such as Lincoln from Washington, Grant, Lee, the Marines at Iwo Jima, all gone without a trace. All without a clue. Maybe they were all with Paul Revere, some pondered. The only good thing about all of these items going missing was the fact that it had people talking about history again and it replaced the overwhelming news of hate and things that offended people.

Washington notices

The Senate and House were like giddy little kids at the circus as they waited for the last of them to be seated in anticipation of what the President was going to say. The rumors in the media told tales of everything from UFOs to an inside plot by Russia to send the country into mass hysteria. Either way, the president promised to deliver some answers and a plan of action. The Senator from Kentucky had been in contact with a young man from his home state who gave him insight into this. Insight that he was sure no one else had the luxury of.

He was not in any hurry to share the information he had and would only bring it up after meeting with the family later in the week. The President, in her usual business attire, moved to the podium and immediately cleared her throat, as if nervous. Nothing to be nervous about, except the country had slid down a razor blade during her administration, right into a pool of alcohol.

Everything about her administration was in disarray. Her Secretary of Defense and Health Secretary had both resigned.

Gas was at an all-time high, allies of the U.S. as well as the U.S. had allowed refugees into the country at an alarming rate, without any scrutiny, and background checks, nothing of the sort. Now these refugees were perpetrating attacks on the citizens of the host country and the world was very angry.

The world looked to her administration to lead, not shy away from a fight, which was what she had done the first six years after taking office. Many soldiers had died because of her deception and inaction, and it was starting to catch up to her. Her advisors told her that this was the biggest speech of her life and that her legacy depended on how it was received.

As she organized her papers for a few more seconds to gain her composure, she looked out into the crowd, making eye contact with many supporters and foes as well. They were going to be tough to tame, but not as tough as the millions of people around the world. She had faked her way through this presidency and now it was time to fake yet another crisis.

Two hours later, after many boos, and a few rounds of applause, she was done. No time for questions, she now had to meet with the Joint Chiefs to plan the next step. She had just spent the evening trying to explain the earthquakes, missing bodies, and grave excavations and attempted to deflect questions about the boy with the visions. Bottom line, the U.S. Government was not going to accept anything that could not be explained. It was the work of terrorists, plain and simple.

The Senator from Kentucky knew the President didn't have a clue, which was the way it needed to be at the moment, for the safety of the boy. "Senator, I have someone that would like to speak with you." His aide had allowed a priest into his private chamber, not allowed under current security measures, but he would deal with him later.

"Can I help you, father?" He asked as he moved the father to the side of the room.

"This is unusual. You should not have gained access to this building."

The priest had a concerned look on his face as he handed the Senator a crumpled up piece of paper. Some numbers were written on the paper with one word; 1- 2116 and the word 'Boston.' The Senator waived for his aide to leave and close the door on the way out. "So, father, what do recent events, this paper, and the church have in common? How do you figure into all of this? Are you going to tell me these are acts of God?" The priest touched the Senator on the shoulder and with a stern expression replied, "God has nothing to do with this."

The warning

The Senator and the priest, who asked to be called Father Robert, talked into the night. The priest even had a few beers, and he handled them like a champ. He spoke of the Founding Fathers, the Declaration of Independence, and the Constitution; moving from them to what was to come, a lesson in manners and respect is what he called it. "Our country has gone down the wrong path, disregarding the Bill of Rights, and the safety of its citizens. It has to stop." The pastor stopped to think. "Our leaders forgot what they swore to, and it's just not the One Nation under God bit either." He paused to take another drink. "Our forefathers fought to gain independence from tyranny. The British were caught off guard by our resolve. Now the media and our leaders have lulled the citizens into depending on them for everything from what to watch on TV, what to eat, who to vote for, and the worst thing of all, social media dependence."

What the priest had to say was fascinating; he had such insight on the beginning of the nation, the struggles, and how things had changed for the worst. He stopped short of predicting the end of humanity, but did say the date and word on the paper were significant and could mean disaster, unless something was done to get the country back on track. "Why me, I mean, why not the other leaders, the president even?"

A chuckle escaped from the man of God and he spoke again, "The President will not listen to what I have to say,

Congress will listen, but not believe. You appear to really care about the country. And……" He got a sly grin on his face like he caught someone looking at porn. "You have access to the boy."

Back to Kentucky

Tom checked his bag in at United for the 1730 flight to Louisville. Larry and Ashton were meeting him there, then they were driving to Frankfort to meet the Senator from Kentucky. Tom had a dislike for political figures, but Larry assured him that this one was genuine and would help. Tom walked down the ramp to board the plane and took his window seat, preparing for the quick flight to see his old friend. Before lone he was napping.

The moon shone bright, Tom realized he was near the harbor, but something was not right. Things were different. Gone were the yachts and the speed boats, as well as the houseboats that dominated dock-side parking in the harbor. There was an old boat there now, not really old, but historic, flying a familiar flag, the British flag. Tom saw men approaching from the warehouse area, or what he knew as the warehouse area.

As he got up to see what the men were up to, he stumbled, landing in a water puddle. He looked into the puddle and thought he saw Tonto from the Lone Ranger, but realized it was his reflection he saw. Immediately he knew he was witnessing the Boston Tea Party.

He followed the men as they walked up the gangway to the main deck, a little excited to be witnessing part of history. One by one they tossed the crates overboard, moving swiftly under the cover of darkness. His wife would never believe his story. Hell, he didn't believe it either and suddenly remembered he was supposed to be on a plane to Kentucky. As he exited the boat, he realized that he had lost track of the others. Were they the Sons of Liberty? He thought he recognized a few of them, maybe?

Now he was face to face with a British soldier, possibly the one that should have been guarding the boat during the party. He tried to raise his arms to get by the soldier, but could not get out of the way of the knife that was plunged deep into his chest. He felt the blood gush from his chest, now open and gasping for air, as blood from his mouth spilled down his chin and he fell forward.

"Sir! Sir! Are you ok?" Tom opened his eyes to see a very attractive stewardess bending over him. He must have passed out and hit his head on the seat in front of him. The blood he felt running from his mouth was saliva that he slobbered everywhere. Damn he was embarrassed, especially in front of the hot stewardess.

He managed to sit up and wipe his drool with his hand, managing a weak smile. "Thanks, I'm ok." But he was not. This was his second trip into historical hell and he suddenly didn't like history anymore.

Tom met Larry and Ashton in the terminal. "You don't fly very well, do you, Tom?" Ashton asked.

"I do not, buddy," he grinned sheepishly. "I am glad to

be on the ground." The ride to Lexington was quiet for the most part as Tom revealed his latest nightmare and what he thought it meant. The trip ended with the three of them walking up the steps to the Kentucky Senate building and Tom throwing up halfway up. Rough times ahead, he thought, it was only starting.

The Senator from Kentucky

The office was amazing, U.S. Flags, eagles, picture of servicemen and women on every wall. They were soldiers from around the world, all Kentucky natives. The senator seemed very proud of this. Tom didn't know what to think; his profound dislike of politicians was fading with this guy and it was hard not to like him. There appeared to be no bar, which he found odd. There was no 'I love me wall' which he was sure there would be one. The furniture was simple, yet very sophisticated. It was a very comfortable setting for this meeting.

Since Ashton was the key player in all of this, Larry had him talk first, describing in vivid detail the dreams he had, the people he shared them with, and what he thought it meant. His stories were followed by Larry's concerns and dreams of death as well. Tom was visibly shaken as he told his stories. His stories were particularly disturbing because you could hear the fear in his words and he had moments where he had to pause due to trembling. He appeared to be ill and Larry asked him several times if he was ok. After an hour, lunch, and a few breaks, it was the Senator's turn. No one could have prepared them for what he had to say.

"I'm not a believer in the supernatural phenomena or things that can't be explained by anything other than science." He paused. "However, there are too many things here centered on your son that cannot be explained." He told them of the missing bodies, the missing American artifacts of intrinsic historical value, and then something he was not sure if he should share. "Ashton, they are coming for you. We need to get you somewhere safe. I know a place where they cannot find you. At this moment, they do not know I am involved and that could work to our advantage."

"Who is coming for him?" Larry stood up, ready to defend his son. "Tell me Senator, dammit! Who is coming?" The Senator reached for his phone and coat as he finished. "The President's Task Force, sir. We have to leave now!" Tom grabbed Ashton's arm and motioned for Larry to follow him to the door. The footsteps outside the door alarmed them to the fact that escape was too late. The door exploded open in a cloud of wood chips, smoke, and armed men. The Senator was wrestled to the ground as were Larry and Tom. Ashton was escorted out the door.

It all happened in a matter of seconds. "Senator, you are under arrest for treason and conduct detrimental to the security of the United States." The last thing Larry remembered was the handkerchief that was placed over his mouth.

Audience with the President

The odor of pepperoni was overwhelming. Ashton loved pepperoni, he was very comfortable right now, but not in his bed, or on the couch in the living room. He shifted his focus and saw many famous pictures on the wall, Lincoln, Washington, Roosevelt, and others he vaguely recognized. As he sat up, he felt a hand on his shoulder, "take it slow Ashton, all is ok." It was his dad's reassuring voice. "We are somewhere in the White House."

As he sat up, he noticed that there were others in the room. He recognized dad's friend Tom, but the others were strangers to him. As he looked around dad handed him a Pepsi and a paper plate with a slice of pizza. "Take this, who knows when we will get free pizza and drinks again." It was his attempt to lighten the stress his son was feeling and maybe his own.

They didn't have to wait long to find out what was going on, within minutes the double wooden doors leading to the room opened, and in walked the President of the United States. The two men in the corner stood at attention as she motioned them to sit down. She was handed a plate of pizza and a drink as she moved to sit across from Ashton, Tom, and Larry. "We have quite a bit to discuss, my young friend, quite a bit."

"Where is the Senator," Ashton inquired, "What have

you done with him?" The President smiled and finished the bite in her mouth. "He is not hurt. He just needed time to think. He kept some secrets from us, and didn't tell us he knew you. It's a good thing we listened to his phone calls."

"Can you get to the point, your majesty? You have detained us without due process." It was Tom, always the cop, not afraid to speak his opinion. "Get to the point your worshipness!" He grinned when he said this line; he always wanted to say it. It was his favorite Han Solo line from Star Wars. Larry and Ashton could not help but to giggle a little and stopped when they saw the expression on the President's face.

"This is a matter of national security, so whenever the three stooges are done, we will continue." The three fell silent and gave the President their full attention for the next hour as she explained what she referred to as the "dire political situation" that she was facing. She started with the earthquakes, the missing artifacts, the bodies of our forefathers that had gone missing, and the panic the media was promoting, talking about the strange boy that was at the center of it all. She wrapped it up with her assumption that this was all cleverly orchestrated by terrorists that had infiltrated the United States and with a little investigation, it could all be explained.

"What about the earthquakes?" A question posed by the boy at the center of all of this, "I mean, you can't control the ground and under, can you?" He looked around the room and continued. "It's a pretty lame idea that terrorists could make all of us have nightmares too. Are you saying they have mind control?" Ashton saw the inquisitive and confused look on the President's face; He found it to amuse him a little and decided against being a smart ass. "Allow me to share our experiences, Madam President."

Ashton had a captive audience, including the video recorder the men in black suits had wheeled into the room before they allowed him to start. He told them everything from the battlefields, camps, and even the eyeball; then detailed the other events he was at, such as the Boston Massacre and the execution of Nathan Hale. His details of death and places were so real that he could feel the tension and angst in the room, even from the guys he assumed were secret service. He then detailed the facts of the others that had been in the dreams with him and the President stopped him in his tracks. "The rest of you had these dreams as well? That is impossible!"

"It's true, your highness," quipped Tom. "We all experienced at least one of his dreams personally." The look on the President's face could not hide the fact that she was not very fond of Tom and his sense of humor.

Larry chimed in as well. "Other members of our family and friends have been involved as well. We do not know what is going on, but I can tell you it is not terrorists, and time to figure it out is slipping away." He took another sip of Pepsi and continued.

"Here is what I have figured out. Corpses of our forefathers are missing, as are the documents and monuments of intrinsic historical value. The earthquakes seem to center around all of these unexplained disappearances. Then we factor in the fact that a handful of us are experiencing these visions, that are of historical events that happened around the time these men lived and documents were forged." He paused to gauge the reaction to his words so far.

"This is not a terrorist-led, evil plan to destroy us. It is the forefathers of our country, reaching out from beyond to a country that has lost sight of God, the principles our nation was founded upon, and it is a warning for us to NOT forget where we came from! We need to take our country back from the lifelong politicians who have lost focus on their oath of office. We need to take our country back from the whining, offended every damn second special interest groups that line their pockets. We need to take our country back from you, Madam President!" Larry stopped as the secret service dudes stooped up.

The President looking surprised at the bold comments, ordered the thugs in black to have a seat, and they did.

"Well sir, you have the right to your opinion, and that is the freedom of speech giving that to you. I think maybe you need some professional help, but that is not up to me." She stood up. "Escort these gentlemen to the gate and arrange for them to get back to the airport. Oh, just a word of advice, do not share your freakish beliefs of forefather zombies and the supernatural to the press or I will have you arrested, understand?" Tom, Larry, and Ashton nodded in agreement as they were escorted to the door. "I mean it, not one word!"

Wow, the inside of the White House Ashton thought to himself as they were led to the rear of the building and placed into a waiting car. He could not help but wonder how long this would be a place of leadership and hope.

His faith in the leaders of the country had faded to almost nothing; the only hope left was the Senator from Kentucky.

The flight

Ashton fell into a deep sleep as soon as he buckled in for the couple of hour flight back to Kentucky. It was weird that the trip started in Louisville, picking up Tom, then the drive to Frankfort, only to be secretly whisked away to Washington by who knows what means, now back on a plane. It had been an eventful day, wait though... it had been two days since they met Tom. Where did the time go? The last thing he heard was his dad and Tom ordering a drink from the stewardess as he slipped into a peaceful sleep.

The screen flashed the message 'Please silence all cell phones and respect fellow moviegoers.' Weird, he thought, why are we at the movies? He realized he was the only one in the theater. He was scared, but wanted to see what movie was showing. Finally it started. It had Charlton Heston, and Ava Gardner..... It was one of dad's favorite movies; Earthquake from 1974. As Ashton got up to leave, he realized something weird about the movie: it was more modern than the original. Was it a remake?

As he walked down the stairs, he noticed the screen starting to shake; it felt so real. Almost to the bottom, maybe dad was waiting for him outside. The screen started to shake very violently as did the wall he now leaned up against. This was not happening just on the screen. It was happening in the theater. The vents and light fixtures started falling from the ceiling; the chairs came unbolted as the floor started to buckle. The front rows of the theater had been sucked into the ground and replaced by tombstones.

The tombstones gave way to the shaking earth and fell to the side, allowing whatever was buried there to escape to the surface... grasping hands now frantically reached to escape the hell of the theater floor. Ashton had made it to the exit as the ceiling came crashing down. The lobby was empty, no surprise there, and disintegrating right before his eyes. He was just a matter of feet from the door as he felt the hand on his shoulder.

"DAD!" was his first thought. He was there with him, maybe just in the bathroom at the time.

As he reached the glass doors he turned around to pull dad through the door and grabbed the bony hand that was attached to the most hideous creature he could have imagined. He pulled really hard, escaping the grasp of whatever that was and fell through the door, scrambling to get clear of the crumbling building. He got one last look at the thing that held him in its grasps; it was strangely familiar, the face, though decayed and maggot-infested, showed wildly demonic eyes, and the weirdest part of it was the mustache it still had.

It was a short, horribly butchered mustache that was but a little piece on each side of his nose. The steel and concrete of the building swallowed his assailant as he rolled away from falling debris and into the parking lot. Not fast enough, though, a piece of concrete hit him on the left side of his head. He felt the blood as he started to pass out, but not before he realized where he was, or was not, maybe. He wasn't at the movie theater; he was outside of the U.S. Capitol Building. He also realized who, not what, had tried to pull him into the collapsing building.….

A decision

Larry and Tom had plenty of time to talk on the flight while Ashton was sleeping. They had a big decision to make; it would be the right decision, but they would talk to Ashton first. The PA system announced landing in Louisville in twenty minutes as a short yet productive trip had come to an end. At least they knew where Washington stood on the events of the past week and knew the consequences of the actions they were considering. "Sometimes you have to do what is right even though it is wrong," was one of Ashton's favorite movie lines, and they were on the edge of living that saying.

Ashton began stirring as the plane started to make its descent into Louisville International. He felt like he had been in a fight, dirty and sweaty, his head hurt like hell, and he really needed something to drink. Dad must have read his mind as he handed him a bottled water he had got earlier from the snack cart. The water lasted all of three seconds, and he could have used another one. Dad reached to pat him on his head and felt the sweat pouring out of his son. "Wow, you are sweating like a fat woman on a stair master, son! Are you ok?" He looked at Ashton as he rubbed his wrists, feeling some soreness and now realizing there were bruises on his wrist and forearms.

"What the hell?" Did you get beat up in your sleep was his first thought and then he realized that very well could be the answer. As Larry pulled his hand away from Ashton's head, he realized it wasn't sweat, it was blood. Ashton told him of the dream and that pretty much decided it. They would have to share what was going on.

The Pastor tells all

Father Robert finished his beer and placed a crumpled five on the bar. He reached into his pocket for the paper with the boy's information. He had decided, maybe at the vodka's urging that he needed to come clean with the boy and his dad and tell them what he really thought. This had to be done before it was too late.

Father Robert walked across the road to the hotel he had been staying at. He only slightly stumbled up the stairs this time. He was getting pretty good at this drunk thing and even though he knew it was wrong, it made him feel a little better. As he reached his room, he reached for the door handle and realized that his door was open. He did not leave it open.

The room was in shambles. The bed overturned, as were the dressers and the nightstands. He knew what they were looking for; the folder with the information on the boy and current events. It was in the nightstand drawer. Why didn't he take it with him? "Dumbass" he thought to himself. Now he was cursing! You've done a one eighty Robbie! Good job! At least they did not take his cell phone. He picked up his phone and dialed Kentucky.

He recognized the voice on the other end as Larry and was relieved to know they appeared to be ok. Father Robert asked Larry to invite Ashton into the room and put the phone on speaker so they could all talk. He also asked them to close the door of the room they were in.

They did not need any interruptions.

As Father Robert prepared to lay it all out for them; he asked them to keep an open mind and to listen until he was done, then they could ask questions.

"So, here is what we know. All over the country there have been earthquakes, mudslides, sink holes, all crazy acts of God that have resulted in many weird occurrences. There have been graveyards destroyed and famous bodies gone missing; there have been historic artifacts that have disappeared without a trace. Our forefathers have been seen in the company of ladies at bars and at sporting events. What does this all mean?"

He paused a second to take a drink of his beer left from the bar then continued. "It means that some crazy shit is going on, and Ashton is at the center of it along with your entire family. Hell, even some of your friends have had visions. That is no coincidence. You are having visions, and I do not know the connection as of yet. I think there is something very bad going to happen and we need to tell everyone that will listen. I am talking catastrophic, end-of-world stuff that Moses couldn't have even imagined." He then stopped for a reaction. There was silence for several seconds before Ashton spoke up.

"Wow, that is hard to take in, Father. Why do you think this centers around me?" Father Robert paused a second before answering." You are having the dreams, and if you are not, you are in them. The dreams revolve around historical events and end in horrible death, usually yours. Now your family is having the same dreams and even their close friends. You have to be the key. You have said you love history and think it is important that it is never forgotten. Things that matter to you have gone missing without a trace. We have to go public with my theory, but you need to understand and accept it first."

Larry cleared his throat, afraid to ask. "Ok, Father, let's have your theory," Father Robert finished off the last sig in his bottle and then let them have it. "Our forefathers have chosen Ashton, because of his intense love and deep respect of our history to carry a message to this nation's leaders. A message that will not be taken seriously but for a few; a message of warning that will save our nation and get it back on the right path; not a path of God per say, but a path of greatness that we once experienced. Our forefathers are behind this, they are using Ashton as a vessel to facilitate the message."

"The visions were so violent in nature that they spawned the earthquakes. The earthquakes have freed the spirits of the forefathers and the missing historical items are in a safe place for protection from the impending punishment." Larry and Ashton were silent and the Father took this as his cue to continue.

"Yes, I used the word punishment. Our country has

become so unfeeling, unpatriotic, and so full of hatred that it has come to this. Our leaders no longer support the Constitution, the Bill of Rights or the Declaration of Independence. We care more about offending one person than we do about what's right for America. We care more about allowing "confused-gender" males into the ladies' room than we do about our veterans and elderly. Our veterans commit suicide at an alarming rate and many are homeless. All this while we have a nation of entitlement-hungry beggars who are looking for their next handout. God knows they won't vote for a qualified president. They are afraid to work for a living and are scared their free ride will be over."

"Then there are the notes. The one has a date 1- 2116 and the word Boston. The other had three words scribbled on it: we the people. These notes mean something. But there is more. Those notes and all of my files on recent events were taken from my ransacked hotel room. That means we have an enemy, and they know who we are. We have to act now, go public with what we have before it's too late."

They all agreed that going public was the right choice, but how? The networks would laugh, the papers would as well. They had to find a way to make people listen. Larry knew exactly who to contact.

The Deal

The Senator from Kentucky was more than happy to help Ashton and his family reveal what was happening to the American population. He had to find a news outlet that would let them tell the story their way and not try to put a Democratic or Republican spin on it. That would be the tough part. CNN and MSNBC were out, couldn't get a truthful story out of them to save your life. Fox News was an option; however, the mainstream media had the world convinced that they were Satan's News Outlet.

The only real choice was to pirate the major networks during primetime. For that, he would need expert help. Help from an old friend. The choice was made; it would happen tomorrow night, eight in the evening. Even if it meant interrupting American Idol.

The Senator's old friend was more than eager to help out. He graduated from MIT at the top of his class, but instead of a big, fancy, lucrative paying job, he chose to run a local Internet Company just outside of Bethesda, MD. He made enough to pay the bills and was happy, but friends and family always questioned his lack of initiative. He was eager to stick it to them during primetime.

On November 21, 2015, at 8:02 Eastern, 5:02 Pacific, America lost its mind, especially the East Coast. American Idol had just started and was going to announce its winner on Fox. Grey's Anatomy had a new episode on, as did the Big Bang Theory and DC's Legends of Tomorrow. Instead, they all got a young boy, a politician, a half-drunk priest, and someone's living room in Kentucky. Quick, order Dominos.

The Senator introduced everyone and apologized for interrupting everyone's evening. He then proceeded to tell the incredible story of the quakes, missing bodies, gone astray artifacts, and the reason behind all of it. It took all of 30 seconds for every phone line on the East Coast to light up every TV station up and down the eastern seaboard. The show was on. The impromptu address took all of five minutes, and they begged the country to listen, to know that on Jan 21, 2016, something bad was going to happen, and the East Coast was the target. The warning fell on deaf ears for the most part and the outrage had just begun.

Back to Washington

The switchboard at the Whitehouse was lit up like Iraqi military vehicles trying to escape Kuwait when the US-led coalition started the bombing effort to remove them from Kuwait in 1990. Every light was lit, every phone was ringing, and everyone was awake. Curse words and name-calling was rampant with callers complaining about everything from missing their show to the government trying to scare everyone into giving up the free stuff they had "earned."

The news traveled fast, not like Ashton and the Senator had hoped, but the news of the morons interrupted American Idol. Very little credibility was given to the story they reported and very little was reported of it on the news. CNN reported that crazies interrupted Idol, MSNBC called the news story the fairy tale of the century, and Fox News called it an "effort by Democrats" to scare citizens into something or another. The Senator likened it to the song on Hee Haw long ago… 'Doom, despair, and agony on me…deep dark depression, excessive misery…..' he knew something bad was coming and something had to be done.

It was time for him to address his peers and lay it all on the line. What did he have to lose? He would attempt to call a joint session of the house and senate as soon as possible. He would call it a matter of urgency and say that national defense was at stake. That would cut down on absentees and maybe get enough interest to get the word out.

Feathers and Tea

The smell of burning tires or a crew laying asphalt filled the air as he finished his salted pork and bread sandwich his mom had made him. It was a warm, yet breezy afternoon in Boston. Wait! Why was he in Boston, much less eating a salted pork sandwich? He was in the middle of AP English, last he remembered. In fact, he was in the middle of a writing assignment. How could he be in two places at once? He must have fallen asleep, hopefully his friends weren't writing on his forehead or doing other unspeakable things high-schoolers do to each other.

The commotion from around the corner caught his attention. There was laughing, no? Maybe crying? Maybe some yelling? He did not have to wait long to know what was going on. Soon, several men dragged another into the center of the street. The man was covered in a hot, smelly black substance and looked like he just got caught robbing the hen house because he was covered with feathers. 'Tarred and feathered' Ashton thought. That is what was going on here. One of the men pulled out a bottle of some type of brown liquid and started pouring it down the poor guy's throat. It must have been fairly hot because the man winced as he swallowed it.

Ashton also noticed one of the men was carrying a noose, hopefully just to scare the guy. He had witnessed enough hangings already. He actually felt sorry for the guy for a minute. What could he have done so bad to deserve this treatment? He thought he recognized some of the men from history class and the never-ending stories his dad told him about history. There was Paul Revere for sure, John Hancock, and one of the Adams fellows.

He heard one of the men call their object of abuse Mr. Malcom, and asking him how the stamp business was. Then the strangest thing happened. Ashton realized that the man was looking at him, pleading eyes were fixed on him and he could hear the man's thoughts.

'Don't let it happen, don't let them destroy all that was worked for.'

The loud crash and ringing noise brought him back to 2015. He had fallen asleep and someone had slammed his textbook onto the desktop as the bell was ringing. It was only a dream, but not one filled with his death or someone else's as they usually are.

Fox, CNN, and MSNBC – Oh my!

January 6, 2016 AM

Ashton tried to take some deep breaths to calm down, it wasn't every day he was on TV before millions of people and much less interviewed by Megyn Kelly. She had been his favorite, when he watched the news, of course. His interview on three of the top news networks was coming just hours before a joint session of congress to discuss the recent events of the nation, and to address the crazy allegations spearheaded by the senator from Kentucky.

As Ashton, his father, and the Senator from Kentucky sat in the Fox News Channel studio at 1211 Avenue of the Americas in New York, they were hopeful that they would be taken seriously. Joining Megyn Kelly would be Anderson Cooper from CNN, and Alex Witt from MSNBC; all skeptics of the notion that ghosts from the past were trying to warn the U.S. of impending doom.

'Sixty seconds folks' came the voice from the studio manager. 'Get ready.' From the left, Megyn Kelly, Anderson Cooper, and Alex Witt came in to have a seat. Ashton couldn't help but blush a little and give a feeble little wave when Ms. Kelly smiled and waved to him.

Megyn Kelly was at the top of her field. She had secured hard-sought interviews that her peers had fallen short of, several with the top Republican Presidential contender. She was not afraid to share her opinion and ask the tough questions.

The first question right away was, "Why should we believe this wild tale?' Followed by what evidence do you have, and why are you the one having the dreams?

Ashton handled it like a seasoned reporter.

"I do not know why I am having these dreams. The dreams all have a message and seem to coincide with events that have happened on the East Coast. The authorities found clues at the scenes like a date, January 21, 2016, just weeks away. We the people was also found at one site. You can't tell me that it isn't strange that our forefathers are missing from their burial places as are historical items such as the Declaration of Independence and the Statue of Paul Revere. Can you?"

Anderson Cooper interjected, "It is very strange young man, we the press do not report anything we do not have proof of, and we report the facts." Ashton got a sarcastic grin on his face and spoke back with some attitude. "Wow, are you really going there with that lie, Mr. Cooper? We all know you only report what you want, whatever meets the needs of your agenda, and it rarely relies on facts or any kind of research. Matter of fact, you and your peers in the media can and should be held responsible for the situation we are in now."

He paused to see if there would be any response to his

harsh words. The panel of reporters were too stunned to reply, and after all--- nobody talked to them that way. They were respected journalists, after all. Ashton continued, "for years you have told America what to eat, drink, drive, wear, and what to think. You have taken sides with one or two individuals that are offended by something and turned it into national hysteria, followed by the clamoring to change our laws and delete our history from existence. You should be ashamed of yourselves. You are responsible for what is happening today!"

Larry saw that his son was on a roll and decided to let it go. He was very proud at this point. "America is no longer the leader of the free world. We are the butt of its jokes. Where we used to have respect, we have ridicule. We apologize for everything and ask permission to do, when in the past, we did without question. We worry too much about offending each other instead of doing what is right and taking care of each other. We worry more about a man having the right to use the ladies' restroom because he 'feels' like a woman than the safety of our children against pedophiles and perverts."

"We are taking down monuments of our history and flags that offend a few people. Most people recognize these things for what they are, historical items that are meant to remind us of our history, good or bad. But you far-left crooks are more worried about the story and creating a firestorm to keep your stories running for months and years on end. Get my point?"

'Son' interjected Megyn Kelly, 'you are bordering on disrespect right now and I must caution you.....' "I don't give a damn about what you want lady…. (All of a sudden Ms. Kelly did not look very attractive to Ashton anymore). "I care about what is happening to our country, my neighbors and family. I don't care what hurts your liberal feelings and surely don't care about what Washington, except for one senator, who has his head on straight!" He glanced over to the senator from Kentucky. He took that as his cue to take over for Ashton.

"If the media ever wanted the truth," he started with, "now is the time to listen and believe. We are on the brink of something with disastrous consequences, and we must act quickly. Our country was built upon the strength of our human resolve to include God and the Constitution. We have moved towards an effort to destroy both of these. We are allowing special interest groups and minority groups to determine the path of our country. This path includes ignoring everyone's basic rights, the freedom of speech and religion; the right to have an opinion on something and not be ridiculed because you do not agree with someone."

"For example, if you believe in traditional marriage, you are a bigot. If you believe that the Confederate flag is a valuable part of our history, you are a racist. If you believe men are men and women are women, you are a sexist or something worse." He paused.

Ms. Kelly attempted to say something but the senator cut her off. "I am not done yet. Wait your turn please. The bottom line is that we have lost focus on each other and our country. We are so worried about what we are offended by that we are eroding where we came from. Of course, slavery was bad, but we did not start the slave trade. It was started in Africa, and we allowed it into our country, for that we have atoned. However, it does not give anyone the right to take down statues, burn flags, and erase our history. How dare you try to do that."

"Now I believe that forces from our past, maybe our forefathers are reaching out from beyond the grave in an attempt to get us back on the right track. As Ashton has said, it is all connected together: the dreams, the disappearing corpses and items, the quakes that center on these areas. It is all related. We need to change our ways. I plan on going before a joint session of Congress yet again to demand a resolution confirming our belief in the Constitution and the Declaration of Independence. It is a start. It will also confirm the need to keep 'One Nation under God' in the pledge of allegiance and on our currency. It will keep our history in the schools and not allow it to be erased by those it offends. If it offends thee, pluck out your eye."

"I will introduce this resolution, and we will vote. I do not have much faith in my peers to do the right thing. I am hoping for the best and we will see. Thank you for listening and God Bless America." Just like that, it was over. They did not give the liberal media a chance to dissect what was said nor have much rebuttal time.

The joint session

January 6, 2016 PM

The Senator from Kentucky had managed to get most of his peers together for an emergency session – the thousands of letters and calls, protests from every group imaginable, from church to welfare recipients that thought this was a government plot to take their entitlements, to crackpots just waiting for the mothership, had all created the sense of urgency he was hoping for. He knew that his peers had just watched the interview they did on live TV and could feel the nervousness all around him. He would have to be firm and it was going to be tough to beat Ashton's performance just minutes ago.

As he walked into the House Chamber to speak, he thought this may be the most important speech in his life. He started with a little about himself: "I am from a part of the country that loves god, the bible, and its country, which believes marriage is the rock that made this country great. This country was built on faith, the constitution, and family, just saying that our country has lost focus of what it was built on, instead of trying to erase our history, we should have been learning from it."

"Our leaders have taken money, favors, and bribes from special interest groups. Mostly, all of them have forgotten what they swore to. To uphold the Constitution of the United

States." He paused for a drink of water before he continued, "George Washington always said that the Constitution is the guide which he would never abandon. How many of you can say that?"

He looked around for response, none as usual. "A good friend of mine told me that he believes that America had much greatness left in her. Anyone believe that, as I do?" There were a few hands this time. "Thomas Jefferson, in writing the greatest document ever, stated the following…'We hold these truths to be self-evident: that all men are created equal, that they are endowed by their Creator with certain inalienable rights, among these are life, liberty, and the pursuit of happiness.'

"How many of you agree with that?" He was surprised at the sea of hands that went up. "I am glad to see this. So, the question is this." He intentionally paused to build up the question. "Why do we let the interests of a few influence our decisions? Why do we cater to anyone that is offended, no matter what the reason?

Why do we belittle those who love this country and want to see its foundations stay in place?"

"Why do we have so little respect for the Declaration and Constitution? Why do you disrespect the foundations of marriage if we don't agree with the new look of marriage? Why do we take from our seniors and veterans to build things we don't need that cater to the few? Why do we need to take down all of our historical monuments and hide our history books just because it offends you?" His voice was raised now and anyone who knew the Senator was aware that he was just getting started.

"Why do we give so much attention to celebrities and make them man or woman of the year just because they changed sexes? Why do we ignore the good cops and just bring the bad ones to light? Why is it ok to kill cops now?" He now was pointing to the crowd, in no certain direction. "Have you had enough? Why do we let the media tell us what to think, what to do, and what to say? I know why! Because you don't give a damn, you only care about what America can give you! You know where that gets you? It gets you 'We the people' and 'Jan 21, 2016'."

"Abraham Lincoln once said, 'I am a firm believer in the people. If given the truth, they can be depended upon to meet any national crisis. The great point is to bring them the real facts.' Well, I am bringing you facts that you are choosing to ignore! We have events unfolding all around our great nation, most of them that we cannot explain. Well, I have the answer for you, if you care to forget about your petty life and uphold your constitutional oath to those that elected you!"

The Senator went on to explain the notes found at the sites, the missing bodies and artifacts, the visions that others outside the young boy from Kentucky had, and the events that unfolded with the pastor and the President herself. He concluded with, "we need to take this seriously; our forefathers are warning us to get back to the basics that they built this country on; the Constitution, Declaration of Independence, and looking out for our fellow man, without yelling racism or prejudice, just because we don't all see things the same way. I propose we meet again first thing tomorrow morning to hash out a plan to get this country back on its feet and not at the feet of the world."

The next day, he introduced a resolution to confirm the belief in the Declaration and Constitution as well as the need to keep 'One Nation under God' and 'In God we trust.' Now we wait for the vote, he told himself.

Washington speaks to the people

January 7, 2016

The joint session of Congress met the next day at 12:00. For the first time in decades, there was no one absent. The Senator from Kentucky introduced the resolution calling for a vote of confidence in the Declaration and the Constitution, as well as the use of God in documents, the pledge, and on currency. After his impassioned plea for passage, the floor was open for opposing views before the vote. It was three hours before they were done and ready to vote on the fate of the country.

Outside the session, thousands of protestors had gathered, many with homemade signs. Most were against the resolution, calling it a slap in the face for human rights and concerned about losing what they were getting from the government. They were afraid that the special treatment they had received over the years would be taken away, or worse yet, they would have to work for a living. Some were there in support of the resolution, but they were far and few in between.

They did not stay long because they were called traitors, racists, bigots, and other names that came with not following everyone else opinions. There were even a few instances of violence against the resolution supporters, beatings, cigarettes tossed at them, drinks poured on them, and even spit spewed at them because of what they believed. Of course, all of this was covered by the media with a spin against the resolution.

In other cities around the United States, not just those on the East Coast, the same protests with the same results. In Seattle, police arrested several of the supporters of the resolution for enticing the crowd to violence because they carried a sign that said, 'One nation under God.' Several anti-resolution protestors looted a church and synagogue while police stood idly by.

The results of the resolution introduced by the Senator from Kentucky to affirm the belief in what our forefathers had fought for was: in the House 136 for, 299 against and in the Senate 45 for, 55 opposed. The senator from Kentucky's fears had been realized. The country he loved was on the verge of disaster and there was nothing that he could do about it. His peers, both Democrat and Republican, had sold out, disregarding the oath they took before office.

A California Senator had introduced another resolution, calling for the vote of no confidence in the Constitution and a resolution to reform it based on today's values. He did this just as the vote on the resolution was being tallied up. The Senator from Kentucky tried to oppose it, but was told to sit the hell down and let democracy take its course. The final tally in the House: 300 for, 135 opposed. In the Senate, it was a little closer 56 for, 44 opposed.

The leadership of Washington had spoken, no faith or support for the documents and beliefs the country was founded upon. No concern for the fate of the United States, nor what could happen because of this resolution. It was now up to fate.

6.5 Boston

January 11, 2016

The rumbling sounded like a fat man's stomach after an evening meal of Nachos Grande, some pizza rolls, and a six-pack of Schaefer's Beer violently tossed together prior to an all night stay on the porcelain god. All major cities up and down the east coast felt the quake as it rolled back and forth along the coastline for 13 minutes tossing things around like they were weightless. Boston was a hot mess, Logan Airport, just east of the city, was nearly leveled to the ground with planes tossed around like Legos, and the main tower lay on its side, with a giant gaping hole running parallel to it.

The nearby airports of Beverly to the north, and Hanscom Field to the west; as well as Norwood Memorial Airport to the south were also devastated. If nothing else, the latest quake did not discriminate between the large and small facilities. Size did not matter in this case.

The Port of Boston, its cruise ship terminal, bulk and container cargo facilities, as well as other facilities in Charlestown and East Boston looked like hell had come and gone with several of the biggest cruise ships toppled over to form a dam. The Norwegian Dawn, the Rotterdam, the Veendam, and the Serenade of the Seas, currently home-based in Boston at the oldest continuously operated port in the western hemisphere were on their sides, on fire, and could be seen with passengers frantically trying to escape through windows, over the side, in many case, flailing and screaming as they fell into the frigid winter waters of Boston Harbor.

The port itself was no better. Fires and dead or injured bodies were strewn across the piers. The harbor had not seen this much blood and devastation since the Battle of Bunker Hill on June 17, 1775, during the siege of Boston. The Wharf itself was like an atomic bomb had gone off with mostly everything leveled and in piles of rubble. Bodies and concrete were hideously mangled together in the devastation. Many that were running were crushed by falling buildings or impaled by broken parts of the wharf as it shattered around screaming fleeing citizens. The scene resembled drawings of Vlad the-Impaler stories one would read about in history class.

The Battery Wharf Hotel was a one-story shack now, reminiscent of rural America in places. It once stood majestic, overlooking the neighboring U.S. Coast Guard base and its fleet. The Battery Wharf Hotel and Spa, combining old historical beauty and offering new world convenience was hopelessly lost to include the 54 guests that were still checked in. Hopefully, they were out and somewhere other than the pile of smoldering rubble that remained in the hotels staid.

75 on Liberty Wharf that was known for its brunch, lunch, and dinner selections, as well as its extensive

selection of beverages, had been completely destroyed. Its floor-to-ceiling glass windows, which allowed an unobstructed view of the surrounding wharf, were completely shattered. Luckily, the restaurant was empty except for a few workers. They escaped out into the street until the ground opened up and swallowed them.

The local fish outlet, The Yankee Lobster Fish Co.; famous for its 24 hour delivery anywhere in the continental United States, promising to deliver the "taste of New England" would have to rebuild. From a structural standpoint, it fared better than some of the other establishments. Lobster, salmon, and dozens of other types of seafood carpeted the pier and added to the charred smell of the fires and bodies.

Interstates 90 and 93 looked like trails of rubble after the quake, with thousands of cars crushed and stranded, killing maybe tens of thousands and many more injured.

The last time Boston experienced anything close to this type of quake was in November 1755, mere months after the Battle of Bunker Hill in Boston Harbor. This quake occurred near Cape Ann, and though not severe, it did manage to kill some fish and scare the hell out of the Bostonians. The quake was said to be felt over 200 miles out. This quake was one hundred times worse than that, there were a lot more people and a lot more infrastructure in 2015.

6.5 Washington

January 11, 2016

The nation's capital was hammered as well. The whole area appeared as if someone had dropped an ACME anvil on it. Interstate 495 referred to as the Capital Beltway because it circles the inner suburbs of Washington, looked like a giant crushed pretzel. I-66, I81, I-295, and I-95 met the same fate as the beltway. Travel for emergency personnel was next to impossible, even if they could get out. Cell phone and landline services were down, making the catastrophe even worse. 9-1-1 service was not an option and many of the local emergency services were busy rescuing themselves and their families.

People had taken to the streets to find help, only to find desperation and mayhem. DuPont Circle, with relatively minor damage still had enough for people to take to the streets for help, some to see if they could help others. Of course, there were those who used a bad situation to help themselves to free TV's, groceries, and other items at someone else's expense. This was the normal behavior for some people, and was part of the problem to begin with if you asked people that lived in the more classy neighborhoods.

Anacostia was another place that had its citizens take to the streets for free stuff. The pawn shops, 'now open to the public' as they were yelling while carrying out jewelry, guns, and other items; were a Christmas bazar area that offered the opportunity for citizens to get free stuff. It was a chance for criminals to steal, rapists to rape, and murderers to murder. After all, the local police would not be coming to help, if they helped anyone other than themselves, it would be the rich neighborhoods, away from the ghettos.

The police, in their defense, would shy away from these neighborhoods, as bad as they were during a normal day; it would be suicide to go into those places during a crisis. Adding to the situation was the fact that is seemed commonplace and even acceptable to execute police officers for no reason now. No help was coming to the neighborhoods of DuPont Circle and Anacostia that day.

The major bridges crossing the rivers, such as the Potomac, were twisted paths of metal and death with cars tossed into the river or dangling on the edge; some were twisted into the bridge structures by all the tossing and twisting caused by the quake. It was like a giant human/machine piece of artwork that was hard not to look at. The screams of trapped citizens mixed in with the moans of the injured and dying as aftershocks continued to rumble through the area trapping citizens even more.

As smoke rose to the sky, and screams filled the air, blood ran in the streets of the east coast. Somewhere, someone was saying 'I told you so.'

The quake that shook the entire east coast of the U.S. had failed to affect some of the monuments which some found to be particularly strange. The Lincoln Memorial was unscathed by the quake but something interesting had occurred. The 175-ton Georgia White Marble sculpture was gone from its base with no signs of destruction or movement. Also gone from across the way was Thomas Jefferson, with no trace. Both of these 'big' men were gone. They would not be easy to steal, considering they were surrounded by water. What did they do, get up to take a walk across the tidal basin to smell the Cherry Blossoms?

The Mall

January 14, 2016

In Washington, DC, the citizens that could get out staggered to the National Mall, specifically in the area of the National Museum of American History. The Kenneth E. Behring Center was home to many items, such as the original Star Spangled Banner. The crowd started gathering at 14th Street and Constitution Avenue and was growing by the minute. It is not sure what drove or summoned them to this location. After all, social media was not involved, because without electricity and cell towers, there was no Facebook, Twitter, Snapchat, or any of that other mind-numbing garbage to share information with.

Many of them had homemade signs encouraging the President to listen to the boy and to repent our sins before it was too late. Many of them came in pajamas, some without shoes. It was almost like they were sleep walking. Many carried bibles and rosaries. Many had crosses and symbols of Mother Mary or Christ as a child. It was a religious outpouring of concern that had taken over the mall. Many were reciting scripture, and many singing a hymn.

Unlike the protestors from the previous days, there were few supporters of re-writing the Constitution, very few supporters of the special interest groups that were just looking for handouts or were worried that their entitlements were going to end; and most of all, there was one thing lacking from the thousands of people that had gathered in only about fifteen minutes. –VIOLENCE—

There was no violence. These demonstrators were peaceful, encouraging each other as they asked for their voices to be heard.

Across the road, in the U.S. Capital Building secret bunker, the Senator from Kentucky was listening to a briefing of what was going on delivered by reports from short wave radios and other eyewitness reports. The news was not good: devastation up and down the east coast, millions presumed dead, and all communications and most major infrastructure, including main roads, were gone. It was suggested to have all states mobilize the National Guard, except how would they get to the hardest hit places? He decided to try to communicate with people on NPR, if they could get the word out. They had less than a week until January 21, 2016.

As he was getting ready to leave for the day, he received the latest update on the quake....

1.2 million were counted as dead or still missing, another 1 million injured, and property damage in the trillions of dollars. How could it get any worse?

The Fears of a clown

The Whitehouse was unusually quiet that morning. As the Vice President walked out into the main hallway that led from the sleeping quarters to the offices, he noticed that all the lights were off and that the usual Secret Service guy or two was nowhere to be found. Strange, he thought; maybe the cooking staff was making bacon and they all snuck down there to get a bite.

He couldn't blame them. Susan was the best cook the administration had enjoyed so far. Besides being a great cook, she was the most attractive woman on the staff and the Secret Service agents had a hard time concentrating when she was around. She wore clothing within the staff guidelines, but she looked good in whatever she was wearing. She definitely put the President and First Lady to shame in the looks department.

As he neared the corner right before his office, he smelled the faint odor of cotton candy and something else….popcorn, maybe? As he took a few more steps, the smells got stronger but now mixed with something else; a more putrid, dead smell, and it was the kind of smell that gets stuck in your nose, like that of a skunk freshly creamed by a truck on a backroad. He stopped in his tracks, almost scared to move forward. "C'mon' he thought' You're an old man, stop being childish and go to your office.' He took two more steps forward and his breath stopped in his throat and his heart pounded in his chest. Lightly floating in the doorway to his office was a red balloon. It bobbed up and down, to the left and right, almost as if to mock him.

'OK, you are imagining this,' he tried to convince himself. 'Maybe he watched a movie on Chiller that put these thoughts in his head?' He stepped forward and reached for the doorknob, 'see, nothing at all.' He twisted the doorknob and walked in. His office curtains were open and the morning light made it a little less scary, even with the lights off. Nothing out of the ordinary so far, desk…check….corners and library…check…all was clear. It was then that he noticed his chair was facing the window, away from his desk, as it had been left. He thought it was slowly moving back and forth.

He squinted to see if there was someone in his chair and then got out a feeble "is someone there?" No answer. He moved a little closer and picked up his copy of the King James Bible as he neared the edge of the desk, 'turn around please,' he said with a little more authority. Still nothing. Oh, sure, he thought, knock him out with the bible. He thought that he could now hear breathing and with that came the smell from the hallway. That nasty popcorn, cotton candy smell was now mixed with a smell that reminded him of the breath a drunk would have. He realized that the person in the chair was probably one of the Secret Service guys who had a little too much to drink and had wandered into the office to sleep it off. He suddenly felt a relief rush over him and walked around the left side of his desk to wake that guy up.

He could see the slumping figure of the person in the chair, and even thought he heard them snoring, and reached out to touch the shoulder of the sleeping agent to help him get back to his room. The agent was warm and obviously very sound asleep due to the heavy breathing. A ray of sunlight shone through the office window and he could see the agent's face now. It was red and white…wait, red and white, why was this agent wearing makeup? The agent's head lolled towards him and he could see his face now! It was not one of his agents as he had thought! The face was painted with white makeup and the area around the mouth was painted blood red.

The eyes were painted black and it was wearing some kind of ridiculous costume. As he stepped back, the sleeping whatever-it-was opened its eyes, a glowing red pupil and glowing white everywhere else. It began to get up out of the chair as the VP stumbled backwards to escape the horror of whatever he had just woken up. With his arms flailing and his eyes glued to the hideous thing in front of him; he never saw the body already on the floor and he fell back over it.

The large thing was now completely up and moving his way. He could hear a sloshing noise as it moved towards him. The worst part was the smell, now stronger than ever; it was like a boy's locker room after a football game mixed with a sweet smell of sugary candy. The thing stepped into the sunlight and he could see it clearly now; he wished he hadn't. He could not tell if it was alive, dead, or a little of both. Its white, pasty cheeks hung off its face like it was melting, the red lips were smeared with what he was now sure was blood and makeup mixed. Its eyes were like nothing he had ever seen before. He could not turn away.

Now he could see its mouth clearly, the broken, yellow, blood-stained teeth that hung in its mouth, with pieces of flesh still stuck in between, opening and closing like it was still devouring whatever it had dined on. It was then that he saw it smile, the most nerve-crushing, insane, and faraway look he had ever seen; the eyes of something evil glared at him, almost assuredly sensing his fear.

He tried to get up, but could not. He had finally decided to identify the thing as a clown, but it was not like any clown he had ever seen in any horror movie; this was a clown on steroids.

This clown put Pennywise and the Killer Klowns from Outer Space to shame; it was the most terrifying thing he had ever seen, and he could not get out of its path. As it approached, it evidently was almost done eating as it swallowed some of the fresh flesh that had been stuck in its teeth and was running its slimy, wet tongue over the teeth as if to clean them.

He noticed the clown had a bible; was it his? Did he drop it? The Bible was in its left hand, and in the right hand, a gavel like judges use. This made no sense at all.

Was it a Judge Judy Zombie clown wanna-be? Why was it in his office? What had he ever done? Did the CDC finally screw up and let something out? The clown was almost upon him now, and for all its horrific looks and smells, it must have been a stupid clown because it did not see the body on the floor either.

The clown fell like a ton of bricks and landed flat on him. He was now face to face with his worst nightmare. The last thing he remembered was the smell, the eyes, the hot, horrible breath it was sharing with him, and worse of all…..that slimy tongue that was now licking the side of his face.

The VP woke up in his office, in the chair that the clown thing had been in. He looked around the room, all was quiet, no monsters, and no dead body on the floor!

Whew! Just a dream, he realized. Nothing more, and nothing less. 'OK, get it together,' he thought, 'you have a briefing this morning.' He got up to leave the office, heading to his room for a shower, and suddenly he felt really dirty. As he closed his office door, he felt an itch in his right ear, he reached to scratch it. He brought his hand back from his ear; it was really wet, like saliva wet, and it was covered in red makeup. One detour before the bathroom, he needed a drink.

After he had several drinks, he convinced himself that he had imagined every bit of it and was ready to focus on his job: VP of the United States of America. Being the Vice President in the current administration was a barrel of laughs, not just joking, often thought the current VP of the United States. After all, being a lesbian commander-in-chief had taken her away from her campaign promises; she was so preoccupied with protecting her wife that she forgot what she told the American People she would do. He remembered that his opinion rarely mattered because she was the president of firsts. He had the list memorized….

She was the first female president.

She was the first openly gay president.

She was the first president to refuse to place her hand on the bible to be sworn in.

She was the first president to suggest overhauling the constitution to remove any reference to god and religion.

She was the first president to suggest that the history books remove parts of the history of the American Revolution and Civil War to make place for more important things like the Supreme Court decision to allow same-sex marriage and the decision to allow men that were 'feelin' like a woman' to use the ladies rest room.

She was the first president to declare the Confederate Flag illegal to fly anywhere and to suggest that all copies of the 'Dukes of Hazard' be destroyed. (I am not kidding on that one he always joked to himself)

How could he even have an opinion? It would make him look wrong, like a bigot, or racist, or anti-Semitic, whatever! He felt like he had joined a majority of the rest of the American people who were not allowed to have an opinion if it were not the same as the special interest groups that ran everything. If you sided with the Confederate flag or the Duke Boys, you were a racist. If you did not agree with gay marriage, you were a bigot and at the top of the list to commit a hate crime. If you did not approve of "confused men' using the ladies' room you were a homophobe or something worse.

If you thought gun ownership was okay, you were in a cult run by either Ted Nugent, Charlton Heston, or Donald Trump. Guns are bad, the tool of the devil. They make people commit mass murder. This was the craziest part of the entire administration. They were always making excuses for people. The truth has been ignored for so long he thought, the boy is right, something is going on. He dared not share the dream he had with anyone for fear of being ostracized by his peers and ruining any future presidential aspirations he may have. As he sat in his office, drinking his special cup of coffee, special because of the Kahlua he snuck into it, he drifted off to sleep again.

The taste was heavenly……..

It was the best milkshake he had ever tasted. Cold frosty, the glass was even ice cold. There was even a cherry on top. Where was he? In a bar? No…An ice cream shop! It had pictures of famous people like the Beatles and John

Wayne, movie memorabilia like a Batman poster, and Captain America life-size standups. It was a man cave, he thought, but for geeks. He started to giggle a little and realized that he was not alone. There was a young boy with him, drinking the same drink; he was enjoying the hell out of his as well.

But there was something different about him and his drink. He knew the boy from somewhere, and his drink was not a drink. He stared at the boy for a few minutes, trying not to be noticed before he realized that this was the boy with the visions, the boy tied to the quakes and disappearances of bodies and artifacts.

How did he get here? How did the boy get here? What the hell was up with that drink of his? As the VP looked around he noticed the room changing, much as Ashton did when he had this same exact dream months ago. He noticed that men were approaching their table with guns! This is an assassination attempt, he told himself as he tried to get up. He could not move. It was almost as if he was frozen or tied down.

They are taking me out because I don't agree with their policies; I knew it would end this way! Shhhhhhhhh! Shhhhhhhhh came from across the table from the boy. He remembered now; his name was Ashton from Kentucky. "Just wait for it," he said. "Sit still and watch!" The shadows came into the light, and the VP could now recognize some of the faces: Sam Adams, John Hancock, Tom Jefferson, and

Paul Revere. What kind of dream was this? Why was he here with the beer guy and other old forefathers? The beer guy? He giggled at that but soon stopped when he saw they meant business.

"This is the dream I had when I finally realized what was going on. Look in your drink." The VP glanced down into his drink and was horrified to see a bloody eyeball staring back up at him. He did not scream. Ashton grabbed his hand before he could. "It's ok; I know what it means now! The milkshake represents life, the sweetness of our simple pleasures that we take for granted every day."

"The eyeball is meant to shock us back into reality. It represents seeing the truth I think, still not completely sure. It could also be meant to foreshadow events to come because we have lost our path." He pointed at the beer guy. "These guys represent the path that America should be on, not the one we are taking now. There is still time to fix this, sir." And with that, Ashton was gone...

It was the chirping of the phone that woke him up. It was all of a sudden clear to the VP that everything the boy, the pastor, and the senator from Kentucky had been saying was correct. He had been part of an administration that had taken the country far from its path into a path of lies, deceit, corruption, and debauchery that left most Americans alone and without a voice. How could he have been so stupid? He had helped pass legislation that was meant to erase history, push beliefs on those who did not want it, and to destroy basic fundamentals that were built on honor, freedom, and even the bible. 'At least,' he thought, 'I had nothing to do with that Dukes of Hazard' fiasco.

In God, we trust he thought. That was important to them as well. He was not a bible-toter, but our forefathers were, and that had to mean something. "Mr. Vice President, you know what you have to do." The VP knew what he had to do, but how would he do it to not get them all arrested? This administration had made people 'disappear' if they failed to conform to their way. Of course, he did not have proof, but he knew it to be true. Little did he realize his dream was shared hundreds of miles away.

"Dreams shared are dreams realized" was the thought running through his head. Ashton had just had the same dream as the VP and now had one doozy of a headache. He completely remembered his dream and the VP. He was pretty sure that he asked the VP to join him in dreamland as well. It was all clear to him now what the dreams meant, what the earthquakes meant, why graves were empty, and why things went missing. He jotted his thoughts down so he could share them with his family later, but now he had work to do. He stuck the paper in his phone case and headed out the door.

The edge of revolution

January 15, 2016

The recent quake and new rounds of protests showing solidarity with the senator from Kentucky and Ashton had changed some ways of thinking. (Don't get your hopes up) Nobody in Washington had changed their minds. It was the people who were waking up from their slumber in the land of "my opinion does not matter worth-a-crap-land" and the people who, up until now, had been too afraid to say anything. News reports were slowly allowing these people with different viewpoints to share their opinions, and this was changing some minds about the direction the country was moving in.

Washington's lifelong politicians weren't buying any of it; what did the people know about anything, especially running the country? Some of them thought that 'we tell them what to think, eat, say, and even what sports team to root for.'

A few politicians, like the senator from Kentucky took the lead on getting the word out and trying to reintroduce the previously failed referendum that would confirm belief in the Declaration and Constitution. He had the vote to the floor in just hours. Unfortunately, it failed yet again.

How could they make Washington listen? Progress had been made, but they weren't out of the woods yet. The east coast could not withstand another quake like the one they just had. One more like that and his home in Kentucky would be the East Coast.

Ashton

All the calls had been made, and they were all on their way to Kentucky if time was on their side. He called all of his relatives in WV and begged them to come to Kentucky, where it was safe. How did he know it was safe? He told them that he knew it was and to leave now. His immediate family all lived within 95 miles and were on their way; even Andy took a leave from studies in the UK to go home. There was an eerie sense of calm with his family, not the panic the public was experiencing now.

For some reason, Ashton's words made sense and made everything alright.

Changes to be made?

Despite the efforts to get Washington, as a whole, to listen, it did not work. Some senators and member of Congress advised their respective states to take this threat seriously or to consider at least options to get their people to safety. States like New York and Massachusetts did not listen. Other states, like Maine and Connecticut, expressed concerns that it was too late to do anything, and they would just ride it out.

The Governors of Virginia, West Virginia, Maryland, Delaware, and New Jersey had already declared a state of emergency, though many did not take the danger seriously. Some took it as a reason to loot and pillage; the scene in some cities resembled something you would see in sci-fi movies with all the crazy antics.

The last attempt

Fox News was the only one that granted air time for the senator from Kentucky. It was one last attempt to get everyone to listen to him. As he waited for the word that he was on the air, he said a little prayer to himself.

"Senator, you are life.' "Good evening, my fellow citizens," he started. "The recent events that have unfolded over the last several months have all of us thinking and wondering what is going on; well, I will try to tell you one more time."

"We need to take our country back! The bickering, whining for attention, and pointing the fingers at each other have to stop. We need to unite together to affirm what our forefathers started, to show our faith in the Constitution and the belief that we are 'one nation under God, indivisible, with liberty and justice for ALL,' not just the few! We need to pull together….there are forces at work here that will see to it that we get back on the right track that we……."

The Senator from Kentucky did not get to finish; the lights went out, and the real show was about to begin…… the lights flickered several times and eventually came back on but were dim at best. The senator and news crew realized they were no longer alone in the studio. Dark figures lined the wall at the back of the room, like something from the Twilight Zone or Beyond Belief; they were slow to move but were moving towards the front of the studio nonetheless.

"Who is that there? What do you want? Can we help you?" The figures stopped, all except for one, as the lights became a little brighter. You could have sworn the room was empty. Standing in the Fox News Studio were George Washington, Thomas Jefferson, Paul Revere, Alexander Hamilton, and many others from the birth of America. They said nothing, they had no real look of expression on their faces and made no sounds. Out in front, Washington turned to his right and pointed back to the large green screen area in the back where they just came from.

The screen lit up and began to display images from history; they were not PG images either. Scenes of battle from the American Revolution filled the screen. Blood, guts, bone fragments exploding, brains obliterated by cannon shells, and dismembered soldiers scattered across fields filled the screen. Then from the battlefield to a room filled with well-dressed gentlemen, the scene was from the painting by John Trumball, the signing of the Declaration of Independence. Then back to the scenes of death, followed by scenes of what may have been the first 4th of July celebration.

This seemed to go on forever, but it was merely a matter of seconds. As the images on the screen faded, the bodies of the forefathers started to change as well. They were not fading; they appeared to be melting. Hair was falling out. The skin seemed to be melting away to reveal the skeletal remains of our forefathers. Thomas Jefferson's eyes were hanging from their sockets, dangling around, just held by a tendon and bloody flesh. The screaming in the studio, most likely from Megyn Kelly, did not slow the process unfolding live on national television.

The bodies continued to melt and disintegrate until just a pile of bone and oozing pus remained for all except George Washington. He pointed to the cameras, then to the piles of steaming remains on the floor, and then back to the cameras. Just like that, he was gone, and the Senator had the floor again. After a few minutes, to get his thoughts back together, he tried to continue.

"I find myself at a loss for words here. I don't think I can top whatever that was. It is evident, however, that our forefathers were trying to tell us something. One thing for sure, if you are watching, this was not part of a 'show' or performance. This was not planned. We need to do something before it is too late. I urge you to pick up the phone and call your representatives now; it is probably already too late. Good night, and God bless America!"

Just like that, the Senator was done, never getting the chance to finish his speech, never getting to plead his case, interrupted by what appeared to be the spirits or ghosts of America's founding fathers. The images left no doubt as to what they were trying to say, "death to America." We are on the wrong path. We fought to gain freedom and then joined together to create and sign the Declaration. His parting thoughts were, 'Now we have turned our backs on all that was fought for, and now we would pay the price.' It was time to go home to Kentucky.

Jan 21, 2016

It was two in the afternoon in the nation's capital and so far nothing. Sure, the streets were a little quieter due to less traffic, some businesses that closed, and the few thousand people that left town. Many areas were still roped off from the quake that hit days ago. But even the threat of catastrophe did not slow down the juggernaut that was Washington, D.C. Business had picked up in some areas, mainly the flower and funeral business; all sporting events had been canceled, the Ravens and Redskins opted to cancel home games for a few days and instead played those games as visitors in California and Washington State against the Chargers and Seahawks.

In Boston, hardest hit by most of this, the streets were quiet but not dead. For the most part, businesses were open, and life went on, even with some concern that was shared by the state's leaders. Boston Public Park, usually full of runners, walkers, and people walking their dogs, was unusually quiet today.

Another false alarm was the thought starting to cross everyone's mind as the day wore on. Another quack prediction to the end of the world. References and comparisons were made to that crazy church guy who predicted massive rolling earthquakes that would destroy the world and bring about the return of Jesus Christ, of course, never happened. The President was consulting advisors if she should go on National TV and put an end to all of these predictions of the end.

The rest of the world was looking and starting to point fingers and laugh as well. BBC Network called the reports of the end 'bloody preposterous.' Japan's NHK World likened it to 'Godzilla reports' and Al-Jazeera Network called it a 'Blasphemous lie created by the American Puppet Master to control its people.' Once again, the world was laughing at the panic in America's streets and the ineptness of the democratic system.

Matthew 24:36-37--- "No one knows about that day or hour, not even the angels in heaven, nor the Son, but only the Father. As it was in the days of Noah, so it will be at the coming of the Son of Man."

Then came the rumble from deep in the bowels of the Atlantic Ocean. It was 3:16 PM, fitting in a biblical reference, that the time matched what was probably the most famous verse in the bible.

The hole that opened in the Atlantic was beyond comprehension. Everything living or dead, fossil or rock, was obliterated as it was mercilessly sucked into the dark abyss. The hole resembled the grinning mouth of Satan as it appeared to open wide to swallow millions of screaming souls all at once. The entire ocean floor seemed to roar as the ground shifted, and the ocean floor, once serene and peaceful, took on the look of a hellish battlefield caught in a crossfire of destruction.

As the ocean floor was sucked into the center of the earth, there was suddenly no room for rock, lava, and matter already there to go; it had to go somewhere.

Rock, lava, and everything else residing below sea level was blasted from its home and sent barreling in a mile-high, hundred-mile-an-hour wall of water, rock, and fire towards the east coast of the continental United States. In this beast's path were the major cities along the eastern seaboard of Norfolk, Charleston, Wilmington, Philadelphia, Washington D.C., Baltimore, New York, and Savannah. All totaling over 112 million people, mostly going about their daily business.

All were unaware of the death event about to unfold in mere minutes. The buoy alarms went off, registering the sudden rise in the water level as frantic emergency services, those paying attention enough to notice something was amiss, scrambled to get the alarm out to the public. If lucky, they could save a few lives.

Unfortunately, Lady Luck was out of town this week, and her cell phone was off.

A President in Peril

"Madam President, we have a problem; we must get you to safety." The secretary of defense continued, "There is a mile-high wave of water heading towards the east coast; we need to leave now!" The President looked quizzically at her trusted aide, "Which part?" was her question. "All of it, ma'am!"

As she was ushered out of the Oval Office, she turned for one last look. Would this be the last time she was in here? She pondered. Did she make a mistake not listening to the Senator from Kentucky? She grabbed a family photo on the way out. And a camera that still had pictures from their vacation on Martha's Vineyard this past summer. "Is my wife in the air?" She asked the young secret service agent to her left. "Yes, ma'am, she is." She walked down the steps into the corridor that would take her to Marine One, maybe for the last time.

As she boarded the VH-3D Sea King, she thought about her wife and all they had been through. The media scrutiny they had gone through as the first same-sex couple in the White House. Sure, they had set a precedent, but at what cost? She wondered at times if it was all worth it. The ridicule, strange looks, the refusal of world leaders to visit the White House. Maybe if she had married a man like her parents pleaded with her to do, she would have been a better leader, and maybe, as farfetched as it was, she may have had more insight into what was going on around her country instead of protecting her loved one.

Stop being silly, she told herself; you did the best job you could under the circumstances. You were the first openly gay president; you did a great job. Then she heard a little voice inside her head that told her. "It didn't matter who you were married to. You were a horrible leader." Those words really stung! Horrible leader replayed over and over in her mind. She was so intent on these words and her thoughts that she did not hear the loud yelling from the highly trained Marines in front of her. Her thoughts had taken over, and she was no longer aware of her surroundings.

As her transport lifted off from the Whitehouse front lawn, she looked out the window at what had been her home. Would she ever see it again? What was going to happen to her country? Where did she go wrong? Did she let emotions take away from her ability to run the country? She noticed the wind picking up outside and hoped they had not been too late in leaving. Her last coherent thought was, 'God help us all.'

The school-girl shrieking sound of horror emitting from the Marine pilot's mouth told her something was wrong. She looked out the front of the helicopter and saw what he was looking at: the wave of water carrying telephone poles, maybe some cars, farm animals, and perhaps she saw a school bus? It was barreling at them as they made their attempt to flee the grounds. The water hit them broadside and pushed them back into the front of the Whitehouse, causing an explosion of water, fire, body parts, and concrete. The wave swept across the area with such a destructive force that it was over in seconds. The remnants of what was once Marine One roared on top of the water by the Washington Monument and into downtown Washington, D.C.

It came to a Shore

The recently peaceful Atlantic Ocean was void of sea life today; there were no dolphins, no whales, and no birds at all. The quiet was replaced by a slowly increasing roar and the rising of the water. The roar continued to increase as the water rose and the wave strengthened. The roar was like 100 freight trains rolling downhill; the brakes had failed, and the conductor had jumped out long ago as the massive wave of death barreled down on the eastern shoreline.

Any boat, such as the Lars Von Steuben, a small Norwegian fishing trawler out of Alexandria, Virginia, that was unlucky enough to be out fishing that day, was completely disintegrated by the wave and became part of the liquid beast that was racing hell-bent towards the east coast. Lars, against the better judgment, the better judgment of his wife that is, decided to take the boat out for some afternoon fishing. His first mate Keith joined him for what was supposed to be an afternoon of fishing and cold beer.

They had just opened their second beer when they noticed the water rising on the distant horizon. "What do you reckon that is Keith?" Lars asked. "A mirage thingy?"

Keith shrugged his shoulders, "no idear," was his response. Keith wasn't the smartest of first mates, but he was loyal. They did not have to wait long to find out what it was. A mere six seconds later, they were swallowed by the wave.

Guess he should have listened to his wife.

The rumbling came like a train leaving the tracks and crashing into a nuclear power plant. The quake, measuring 9.1, was merciless as it started in the Chesapeake Bay, rocking its way inland towards the Delmarva Peninsula. The Chesapeake Bay Bridge from Sandy Point to Kent Island was no match for the rolling freak show of water; neither was the Chesapeake Bay Tunnel that connected Virginia Beach to Cape Charles as it crushed the cars traversing home or to play like aluminum cans.

It took mere seconds to cross the 30 miles to reach the mouth of the Potomac. It steamrolled inland towards Norfolk, Newport News, Baltimore, Frederick, Hagerstown, Martinsburg, Lancaster, and Harrisburg as far as Lynchburg, VA, and Altoona, PA, rolling northward towards Manhattan, New York City. Long Island, Trenton, and south towards Raleigh, Wilmington, and Charleston, SC. There was nowhere safe.

Washington – Gone!

The National Mall was all but deserted when the 200-foot-high wall of water swallowed everything faster than a pig eating bacon. There were no joggers, no picnics, and no balloon animals to be seen. The Smithsonian Museums, Washington Monument, and Lincoln and Jefferson Memorials are gone. The memorials to all wars fought were ripped from their once solid foundations, as was the U.S. Capital building. The area between 7th and 14 Streets, usually used for staging parades, is part of the Atlantic Ocean.

The U.S. Supreme Court building, Library of Congress, National Archives, Ford's Theater, and Union Station were no more. The Martin Luther King Memorial, the United States Holocaust Museum, and the Bureau of Engraving and Printing had all met their demise at the feet of the monster wave.

Philadelphia – Gone!

Philadelphia, the largest city in the Commonwealth of Pennsylvania – also an important city in colonial times was chock full of historical places and documents, many of which had disappeared lately, with the governor calling on the ball-less thieves to return the items at once. Today, none of that mattered; almost the exact time the wall of water rolled into town just to the south, it said hello to the 'City of Brotherly Love."

Like Washington, Philly had managed to get many of its people not killed in the quake, to freedom. There were some, however, that refused to or could not leave for one reason or the other. Now, they were entombed there forever. Sites like Brandywine Battlefield, Fort Mifflin, Independence Hall, the Historical Society of Pennsylvania, and Valley Forge National Historical Park were all under ten feet of water.

Boston – Gone!

Once home to 4.7 million plus people and the 10th largest metropolitan area in the country, Boston was founded in 1630 and was one of the oldest cities in the United States. Today, it was a lake. The most historical site in the country, home of the Boston Massacre, the Boston Tea Party, the Battle of Bunker Hill, and the Siege of Boston, was no more. Boston had been home to firsts such as the first public school, the first subway system, and the first public park.

A tidal wave of death and destruction moving at hundreds of miles an hour erased all of that history that the current administration was trying to erase and replace with garbage. Nature had done it for them. Now you could see (if there was anyone alive to see) red bricks from the Freedom Trail and other public areas floating on top of the still-rushing waters. Remnants of the Bunker Hill Monument, tombstones and cadavers from the Granary Burial Grounds, gray siding from the Paul Revere House, and the sign from the Old North Church were washed into the swirling chasm that used to be downtown Boston.

Norfolk – Gone!

What was left of the U.S. Military had left Naval Station Norfolk to head out to see, as well as NATO vessels leaving the Strategic Command Headquarters.

They didn't get too far when the wave sent them flying like a Battleship board game at the hands of a bad loser who had tossed the game after losing. Hampton Roads was leveled, Sewell's Point was leveled and twisted into all of that mess were highways, bridges, tunnels, along aircraft that never made it out of the hangars.

Anyone who was alive during the attack on Pearl Harbor would have likened this to the same level of devastation, maybe worse, except there were no incoming Japanese pilots dropping bombs and going all Kamikaze on American targets in the Pacific. "A day of infamy' was still dead here, but there were supernatural forces at work here, not the enemy.

Every major city east of the Appalachians was leveled and under anywhere from ten to fifty feet of water. The water and devastation rolled westward until it was stopped cold at the 1,500-mile stretch known as the Appalachian Mountains. Of course, there were areas that water was still able to get through, but for the most part, the wave of death was diminished to a few high waves carrying debris, bodies, and metal into the valleys on the other side of the mountains.

Back in Kentucky

The Senator from Kentucky and his family moved inland, back to Kentucky, as did some of the Senators smarter peers, who were invited to bring their families to his retreat for safety and to meet on the situation. The priest had just finished with a prayer accompanied by those who would join him and barely got the 'amen' out before he heard the commotion from the living room. He whispered another small prayer to himself before heading to the television.

They were sipping iced tea when the breaking news interrupted a story on Kentucky Basketball….. Boy, did he hate being right,` the Senator thought to himself. He was fairly sure his home was safe because the priest had told him the mountains would stop the water and that everything west of the Appalachians would be spared because that was where God's country started.

They watched in horror as satellite and news footage came in, showing the waters lashing up against the mountains and nothing but water to the east as far as the eye could see. It wasn't hard to see recognizable buildings, parts of bridges, airports, cars, and trucks; the water had washed up bodies onto the side of the mountain, dozens, maybe hundreds of them littering the area. It was hard to watch, and the senator motioned for the women to take some of the younger children from the room. Many refused to leave; the horror of what was transpiring had them frozen, and they had to watch.

Many of the couples held their children, and some even started to cry.

You could see small fires in the distance and some up close where the violence of the wave caused explosions as it ripped once immovable objects from their bases.

Things like oil and gas tanks, natural gas pipelines, tankers, and a Disney Cruise ship burned in the distance. It was a hard dose of reality to swallow. Parts of roads with cars embedded in them floated between the small town buildings and big city skyscrapers that now all shared the same space.

What was even a scarier prospect was what it would look like when the waters receded. Would they be able to salvage anything to the east? What about the bodies? Would they be carried out to sea, only to be swept back in by the tide later? Would they stay inland and make cleanup a harder, morbid task? Either way, it was not going to be a job anyone volunteered for. Where would they put all the bodies? What about all of the debris?

A small laugh escaped his throat, he didn't mean it, and he had hoped that nobody heard him; he coughed loudly to play it off. He had a fleeting thought about where to put all the debris, and the first thing that came to his mind was, 'New Jersey would be a good place.' I never cared much for New Jersey; the thought made him feel somewhat ashamed, but he chalked that up to all the emotions that were bombarding him right now.

Soon, the task would start to rebuild. They ask the tougher questions like who is in charge now with the President and VP dead, as was most of the stubborn leadership in Washington dead from either the quakes or the tidal wave. Where would the capital be? Would we learn from our mistakes? What had actually happened here? Was it our forefathers or God? Was it just Mother Nature cleaning the house and taking out the garbage?

These reasons did not account for what happened to all the missing artifacts and bodies over the last several months, did they? Why was Ashton the center of all of this? Why had America gone so far off the path its forefathers set for it? How could we recover? OK! Slow down, he told himself; all would be answered hopefully.

He stepped forward and turned the TV off. He then opened the front door to step outside and enjoy the cool Kentucky breeze coming in from the east over the Appalachians. 'God bless America,' he whispered.

The last dream?

Ashton couldn't take anymore; he was exhausted from all of this. After all, he had been having these dreams for a long time, and everyone thought there was something wrong with him. Now he and they knew better. As he lay down on the bed, he stopped on SyFy channel to watch whatever cheesy show was on.

Cool….Z-Nation Marathon, he might not get any sleep after all. This was his and his mom's favorite show. They even met the stars of it when they went to Lexington.

Comic-Con last year. Most of the cast was nice, especially Kelitta Smith. She was a lot prettier in person, too.

Mom got to talk to her for a few minutes and got a hug. The picture was in a frame in the living room. They had a great time. Before he knew it, he was out…and dreaming again.

The grass was a dark green, green like money, thought Ashton; he knew he was dreaming again, but this time, no fear, no anxiety, and nothing dead- so far, anyways. He could smell flowers and water, as well as something yummy, maybe apple – no…. cherry pie! He loved cherry pie. Now he knew it was a dream! As he walked, he could see water, a river he thought, maybe the Potomac River. He was pretty sure it was the Potomac; he must be on the East Coast, he thought. Maybe Alexandria or near Washington, D.C. He passed a group of trees that he recognized as English Boxwoods and almost immediately knew where he was. They had visited this place many times before when he was younger. Mount Vernon, home of none other than George Washington himself.

He remembered from the tour that Washington built the house around 1758, and it took about twenty years to finish. Washington finished his life there when he died in 1799. He remembered that some ladies' group ran it now, and it was open year-round for everyone to visit. Strange though, he wondered to himself..... His dreams usually had other people in them; he was all alone. He thought he heard some laughter off in the distance and started to worry. This could be where it gets weird, he thought. As he passed a big tree on the left, he noticed a couple of men and a beautiful lady talking by a small table.

"I've been expecting you, young master Ashton," the voice said as the man in front of him turned around. It was President Washington! "We have quite the amount of things to discuss." Ashton was thrilled! His dreams were never this exciting without someone dying. He could not wait to hear what the president had to say. "Mr. President, I am so happy to meet you." He exclaimed. "You can call me George, not the President anymore, you know, and Tom has that honor now."

As they walked along the front lawn in front of Mount Vernon, he noticed some African-American staff and wondered if they were slaves. He knew from history that Washington did employ some slaves and that they were treated as part of the family. He guessed they looked happy but could only wonder how they felt.

They neared the front of the house now, and Washington pointed to some chairs on the porch. They sat down, and the president began to tell a story.

"This must be a shock to you, and I am sorry you had to go through all of this. You see, when we set this great nation in motion, we knew there would be issues to work out. We also knew that as the country grew up, there would be new creations, new ideas, and new ways of doing things that would test and stretch the Declaration as well as the Constitution." He paused long enough to thank the staff member who bought out tea. "That has happened far beyond our imaginations, and there was no way we could have known how much the nation would grow past the thirteen colonies."

"The nation has become a pot of many nations with many ideas and ways of life. We did not foresee that. What I envisioned was an America that the world looked to for its leadership, its values, and its faith in God. But somewhere over the years, all of that faded. The world does not look at us. Instead, they point at us with drunken laughter. "

At this point, Ashton thought he saw the former president tear up. "The basic rights of all citizens are being ignored because our leaders only care about fortune and fame. No one person should have the right to express themselves over others. We have allowed the minority to dictate what the majority does, and if the majority does not think like the minority, then they are crucified and belittled for not agreeing."

Ashton knew this was a dream but couldn't help but be proud to be sitting here listening to the greatest American ever to live. He took a sip of his tea and commented that it was very tasty, which drew a smile from the weary man sitting in front of him. "The right to freedom of speech is gone unless it is a radical view that goes against what most people think. A citizen's sexual preference is their right. However, it is not fair to force it on someone that does not wish to partake in that type of behavior, nor to hold them in ill thoughts because they do not agree."

"Our history is not perfect, we, I, made mistakes, but we were a young country. We overcame the strongest army and navy in the world against the odds, and a new nation for all was born. Instead of growing as a nation, we are growing apart, so scared to offend our brother that we feel quiet and afraid to speak our minds. That was not the intent. It was also not the intent of the representatives of this nation to make a lifelong job of political service either."

"We learned of the evil of slavery, and eventually, through a terrible war, it changed. We saw a man, with the idea of a super race of humans, destroy half of Europe before he was stopped by a collective of nations. It was sad days we endured, but we endured none the less, and we need to remember this so the same mistakes do not befall future man. If we forget, we tend to make the same mistakes. Do you understand what I mean?"

"Yes, sir. I do." Was Ashton's reply. Mr. Washington continued. "That is why we chose you. You were raised by parents who loved history and considered it important and sacred. They shared that passion with you, and it has grown inside you. I regret how we had to use you in this endeavor, but it was most necessary. The shaking of the ground was to get the whole of the population to pay attention through your media; we regret any loss of life and property, but desperation had grown, and time running out."

"Your current president she loves her country. She had high aspirations of leading it in a great and new direction. She, however, was tied down in her own issues and, like many others in the public service now, was swayed by those who could offer her power and material items. She got caught up in the wave of those easily offended by things that should be taken for what they are, that would be opinions and freedom of speech. The voices of patriotic, country-loving Americans were silenced by those who sought to destroy the very being of what this country stands for. That is why the earthquakes, the missing cadavers, and the historical items were removed. They were removed for safety and to get the leaders back on track."

He knew Washington was crying now. "But they did not listen. No matter how much destruction, death, and mayhem we inflicted, the majority remained silent except for a few. The few that saw what was going on and had the fortitude to move past the fear of what the few thought. That was yourself, your family, and a handful of others, such as the senator from Kentucky."

"You were chosen to be our voice, the voice of the forefathers. We could have shown ourselves to someone else, but we feared that it would have become a charade and not be taken seriously as it should. The nation was running out of time, almost to the position where it could never recover. There are those who want to replace our history with the history of the few that need to be stopped. History can be defined as the study of past events, where someone has come from, and what they endured. This is a learning event. We learn from our mistakes, which is important for all of us, so as to avoid erring in the same issue again."

"We had hopes that your senator friend, who is deeply concerned about his country as you, had made progress with the vote to confirm belief on our nation, but that failed. We had to try one more time with the quakes, which unfortunately left thousands more dead and much more destroyed. That we are sorry for, but felt it a needed step."

"You and your family endured these dreams and public ridicule for the sake of saving the greatest nation in the world; it's a shame that it took so long to achieve the results.

We would have preferred no one had perished. Do you have any questions for me?" Ashton thought for a few moments, and he did have some questions to be answered.

"Why the terrible nature of the dreams? I was always dying. My friends and family saw me die; sometimes they were hurt during these dreams. I know that there were parts of the dreams that were meant to get our attention, like the eyeball in the milkshake thing, which I normally would have found to be pretty cool."

Washington continued, "You are correct, they were meant to get your attention, and you are such a visual people now, some things you are numb to. The eyeball was meant to open your eyes to the reality that all is not as it seems. It was extreme but effective. Your family was involved because a man will take things much more seriously if his family is affected. The death and injury were to add some reality to the message, which also worked. You are a strong young man, and I am proud to have met you. You and your family have helped get us back on the right track. We would all like to thank you." Washington pointed to his right, and suddenly, they were not alone on the porch. Many other historical figures, both men and women, reached out to shake the hand of the young man who was not afraid to fight for his country. Ashton could only smile because this reminded him of his favorite movie, the one where the two slackers had to get an A on their history report to pass for the year. This was just like that, except no phone booth and no heavy metal band.

He recognized Paul Revere, John Hancock, Crispus Attucks, Betsy Ross, the Adams guys, Benjamin Franklin, and many more. This had been a 'most excellent dream' and had answered many of his questions. He thought to himself as he felt himself fading off to sleep. He would soon wake up at wherever it was that he fell asleep, but this time everything was ok.

Louisville, KY

With the entire eastern seaboard obliterated, the United States needed a new place to operate its business. Many cities were considered, but in the end, the logical person to make the choice was the senator from Kentucky. The obvious choice after Frankfort, KY; already the capital of the Commonwealth, was Louisville. Now, Louisville was far from perfect; they had a record year of crime, with murders doubled over the previous year, but the senator from Kentucky loved its charm and, most of all, its history and knew it would be a good home for the 'new look' America.

Located on the border of Ohio and Indiana, Kentucky's most famous city, founded in 1778 and the oldest city west of the Appalachian Mountains, is Louisville. The home of flavored chewing gum, bourbon, the Kentucky Derby, baseball bats, and Mohammed Ali, Louisville is considered to be a little southern and a little mid-western. It was a melting pot of people and was the perfect place to mend the countries' differences.

The commotion surrounding the choice of Louisville was only made more controversial by the sudden influx of 'men in black' to secure the location of the temporary new digs for the government. The location of choice was located at 140 N. 4th Street in Louisville. More commonly known as the Galt House Hotel, it offers an outdoor pool, a salon and spa, six restaurants, a rooftop exercise room, two ballrooms, and over fifty meeting spaces. Many of the rooms have wet bars and mini-fridges. It wasn't the White House, but it would do for now.

The new kids on the block

"Many say this was a second American Revolution. Revolution is defined as the overthrow of a government in favor of a new system, also a rebellion, revolt, uprising, insurrection, mutiny, and insurgence; in this case, no citizen came to bear arms, there was no militia or redcoats involved." The senator from Kentucky, just sworn in as President of the United States of America, was giving his acceptance speech, flanked by his family and his vice president, who happened to be from the other party. "This revolution was a necessity forced upon us by our history; many stories of strange events have come out, and you will believe what you are going to believe anyway. The bottom line is that we now have a chance to become what our forefathers wanted: a united country, a people of one nation; it doesn't have to be under one God but under one common goal. We need to have each other's backs; we need to respect one another's opinion, even if it is not ours; we need to work together to make this nation great again."

"Together, we can end our hunger, end our joblessness, end our hatred towards beliefs and practices that we do not understand. There will always be those who hate us; we cannot change that. But we can work together, Republican, Democrat, white, black, Muslim, Hispanic, to build this country to what it was meant to be. A nation that will not tolerate crimes against our brother, sister, mother, father, or child; a nation that will think about our actions before we jump to conclusions; a nation that will stand up for our rights and end this ignorant lashing out at each other because we are offended or don't agree. "

"I will work with what is left of our senate and congress to put into place new laws on term limits, new laws on special interest groups, and new laws on the protection of our history, its documents, monuments, and words; we will not forget where we came from. If you do not like what I am saying, then that is your right to have that opinion. But……..and heed my words, if you react to my words with prejudice, malice, or violence against your brother, or sister, or any citizen, you will pay the price. That is not a threat; that is a promise!"

The President from Kentucky thanked the citizens and left without answering any questions. There was much work to do. Many meetings many things to vote on. There were many documents and monuments to replace and try to salvage from the East Coast that were starting to sink into the Atlantic Ocean. His top scientists figured they had a month or two until the Appalachian Mountains were the new east coast. New ports would have to be created, and new military bases to defend the coasts would have to be mobilized. The new America would make many new enemies, some old ones would re-emerge, and some new ones would surface. His new ideas and putting America back out front were really going to piss the world off. "Bring it," he thought to himself with a smile. "We'll leave the light on for you."

Aftermath

It had been months since America had been turned upside down, and things were looking up. The new government had managed to salvage some of the historical items that had not been destroyed and had to give up on some others that were beyond saving. The entire east Coast had slid into the Atlantic Ocean and to the bottom. There was no beach area now, and if you stepped into the water, you would drop at least one hundred feet into a chasm. No more Ocean City, no more Boardwalk, just the deep Atlantic nestled up against the Appalachians.

Construction crews had already started cutting away at the rock to build America's new ports. Places that had never really been home to ships in the past were now being fitted for incoming and outgoing cargo. Several cities, such as Chattanooga, TN, Pittsburg, PA, and Cincinnati, OH, were now being fitted as major ports. It was a lot of effort to realize this, but the work was going well. As far as port security, all of these cities already had some type of military presence, mainly the U.S. Coast Guard; they would just upgrade the bases to support the new mission. Before the events, some were calling it the Rapture of '16; there were the major military bases of Ft. Bragg, Ft. Drum, and Ft. Meade on the army side; Annapolis, Charleston, and Norfolk on the Navy side; and Dover, Charleston, and McGuire on the Air Force side; all erased and under 100 feet of water now. All military bases in Washington, such as the Pentagon, ceased to exist. Many wondered if NORAD and members of Congress who were unaccounted for had escaped to the famous Greenbrier Hotel and its underground bunker; the latest word was 'no.'

Only one reminder of the East Coast remained: 739 miles to the east of the new American Capital, out in the middle of the Atlantic Ocean, one small island remained, spared by the quakes, the tidal wave of death, and the events of the months before. That island, known as Liberty Island, is the home to a crown-wearing, bible-toting lady known as the Statue of Liberty. Somehow, this icon of America survived everything thrown at it. The buildings surrounding it and all the vegetation had been stripped from the surface of the island, but the colossal statue did not budge.

Seven hundred thirty-nine miles away from the Liberty Island miracle, Ashton and his family were taking a few days off to see some of Kentucky, with a final stop at the new Whitehouse to visit the president. The first stop on the trip was Mammoth Cave National Park, known for its grand, gloomy, and vast chambers; it was the world's longest-known cave system, with about 400 miles that had been officially explored. The fifty-mile trip down Interstate 65 to Exit 53 was fairly boring at best, but Ashton took that time to work on his book about his experiences, and then there were the talks of a movie.

He only had one requirement for these: that most of the

money goes to the protection of our historical documents, monuments, and sites. America's history was worth saving, and he would do his part. As he jotted down some ideas, he thought of his college options. He did not know where he was going, but he was going to teach history and science, that was for sure. The remained of the money would go for his college education and to help his family.

As his dad pulled the RV into Mammoth Park, Ashton had a weird feeling that he could not explain. As they ventured down towards the entrance into the cave, they realized that many people were turning around and coming back. As they got closer, they saw why: the entrance was blocked by State and local police as well as U.S. Park Rangers. Not being one to 'not be allowed into Wally World for no reason,' Ashton moved forward to ask what was going on and was met by three Kentucky State Troopers who restrained him from going any further.

"Do you know who this kid is?" asked a gentleman in glasses just feet from the entrance. "Let him and his family pass," he ordered. Ashton looked at his dad and his dad at him. They moved forward toward the guy who had given the order to let them in. Secret Service, maybe? Men in Black? CIA? This was sure to be interesting, he thought. One thing for sure: the guy looked like no one ever messed with him, probably not even his mother. As they reached the man, he put out his hand to Ashton and shook it. "Thanks for all you have done for us, Ashton. I need you and your family to come with me."

Off-limits

As they made their way down into the deep, musty, and dark cavern, Ashton could see lights flickering in the adjacent tunnels leading away in all directions. He could also hear voices, and the shuffling of feet and the rumbling of equipment. He wondered to himself about what could possibly be going on.

"Dad, what is going on here?" He glanced over at Larry and at first thought he saw fear, but he knew better, there were very few things this towering man was afraid of.

"I think they found something, maybe a leak, or maybe they had a cave in. If that were the case, though, I do not think we would be down here." He smiled at his son and motioned for him to keep going. "We'll know soon enough I guess." As they took a few more steps, they could see an entrance into what looked to be a larger cavern and maybe the one with the most activity going on. There was quite a bit of equipment in that cavern as they entered. They could see all kinds of shovels, picks, and other sophisticated drilling equipment leaning up against the cavern walls. "Right over here" the strange man in the suit told them, as he led them to a corner of the room.

They stopped at the base of a concrete slab, kind of a strange thing to find down here, not natural, but manmade Ashton thought. The base was very smooth and had some writing on it. Ashton gasped as he read it and his father soon caught on as well.

IN THIS TEMPLE AS IN THE HEARTS OF THE PEOPLE FOR WHOM HE SAVED THE UNION…it started…

Ashton looked up and realized that the base held a statue. He first saw feet and followed the statue up to the rest of the body and finally a face. The man looking back at him looked weary, as if he had the weight of the nation on his shoulders. His eyes told of a struggle, many had died, many scarred forever. His face was worn and haggard, framed by a beard that many a morning went un-kept and probably at the end was mostly gray. He looked back down at the rest of the epitaph.

THE MEMORY OF ABRAHAM LINCOLN IS ENSHRINED FOREVER. The Lincoln Memorial? This was impossible, how in the hell? Ashton often cursed in his thoughts as all teenagers did, but did not realize that this time it was out loud. He looked around, no strange looks, not directed at him anyway.

"How the Sam Houston hell did this?" That was his dad. There was no way man did this, the monument was flush up against a lower part of the ceiling and could not have been rolled, lowered, or even disassembled and placed here. He looked at Agent 'Bob', since he never formally introduced himself. "What else did you find?" Agent 'Bob' lowered his shades and gave them a come-this-way motion with his head. They turned and headed right into another cavern.

The next thirty minutes answered a lot of questions that millions of people had asked over the last several months. What had happened to the statues and documents that went missing? The answer was simple, they were here in the bowels of Mammoth Cave, in the center of the Commonwealth of Kentucky. Nestled into a cave by some force of nature, or the supernatural. At this point, it was more supernatural than nature.

"This is just like that Nicolas Cage movie," Ashton shared with his father. National Treasure; that was it! But in that movie man moved the treasure from location to location. Man, at least not the living, had nothing to do with this.

The last half hour had turned up missing documents such as the Constitution, The Declaration of Independence, the Magna Carta, the Bill of Rights, the Gettysburg Address, and many others that had gone missing. Paul Revere was in a cavern with Thomas Jefferson, and George Washington, along with hundreds of other monuments reported missing over the last several months. Many of the items could have been carried into the caves, but most of them could not have been. It was a real mystery if you ruled out the supernatural approach to it.

"It's all here," Ashton thought to himself, "everything was saved; but why here, why now?" He made notes of what had happened and pretty much kept to himself as they continued their trip down I-65. This was going to make a pretty awesome book. As the tires thudded on the road, he slipped off into what may have been the best sleep he had in a long time.

Later would come word that all of those historical items were moved to a warehouse off of I-65, of course in an undisclosed location, heavily guarded by the men in black suits without names.

Stuff and things

Wing A of the hospital had been in disarray for years, only paranormal investigators and tourists ever ventured into the empty hallways and rooms of the once-busy mental hospital. Supposedly, thousands of soldiers and crazies had died in the hospital and there had been many television shows dedicated to the hospital over the years. The place was really hopping during the Halloween season with tours and haunted houses every night. There had been talk from the owners about building a hotel on the first few floors and leaving the rest as a haunted attraction, but so far the money and plans had not materialized.

Tonight though, was very quiet, just a slight breeze flowing through the open areas and places where the windows were open or broken. No one roamed these halls, no doctors, nurses, orderlies, custodians, not anymore. As with all hospitals, you had your stories of murders and suicides, strange illnesses, and occurrences throughout the years. The only things moving were the leaves that got in and the bugs and the occasional animal that was seeking shelter from the weather.

Room 232, according to paranormal peeps, was a hotbed of activity. Hangings, wrist-slashing, knifings, strangling, you name it, it happened there. As with any abandoned place, cobwebs had built up, rodents had left droppings, and bugs had over-run everywhere. But room 232 did not look like that at all. It was cleaner, if that's a word, and appeared that someone or something had tried to keep the place up just a little. In the corner, there was a small table, maybe a table for a lamp, it was weirdly out of place in a barren hospital. It was clean as well. On the corner of the table were some papers, slightly blowing from the draft coming into the room.

The papers were actually part of a newspaper, the Boston Globe, it was folded open to the section where people can write letters to the editor, (not that they ever get read), and the one particular letter was circled in red.

If anyone were there to read it, they would see the following from a concerned citizen.... 'Sir, I am concerned about the direction our country is headed in. Our own government spying on us, listening to our calls, conversations, watching our consumer habits, forcing us to take its health care, and placing our soldiers and national defense in peril by negotiating with terrorists and working with countries we do not trust because of their hatred towards us and their policies.

The U.S. Constitution is suffering total disregard by the leaders who took an oath to uphold it. This, sir, is unacceptable. I see our veterans struggling to find work, wondering where dinner is coming from, and hoping that the VA can provide the healthcare they so desperately need. That is no way to thank our heroes and their families.

Our forefathers fought tyranny, oppression, and the greatest military force at the time to gain our independence, and we find ourselves facing the same threats from our leaders, the ones that should be protecting us.

I believe it is not too late to turn it around. Many of our fellow Americans look the other way, not because they don't care, but because they have lost hope. I haven't. I still believe men like you can bring us back to where we need to be. A place where we are not afraid of our own shadow, where we are proud to salute the red, white, and blue, where we are supportive of our men and women in uniform, and where we are quick to defend what our veterans have and are fighting for.

This is about more than Democrats and Republicans, this is about the United States of America, a once proud leader of the free world that has lost its way and left many of its citizens with the hopeless attitude you see today.

Thank you for listening.'

The response was just a few words, from obviously an editor that really did not care....

'Thank you for your letter, please contact your elected representatives about this.'

Also in the pile of papers was a torn photocopy of an old document, the words were blurred but could be read in the light if someone was there to read it...

'When in the Course of human events, it becomes necessary for one people to dissolve the political bands which have connected them with another, and to assume among the powers of the earth, the separate and equal station to which the Laws of Nature and of Nature's God entitle them, a decent respect to the opinions of mankind requires that they should declare the causes which impel them to the separation.' At the bottom of the page. Along the edge of where it was torn, written in marker were the words, 'absolute Despotism.'

Looking out the windows of Room 232, you could feel the breeze, cool and brisk, a constant breeze, blowing through the window into the hospital; the rain was getting heavier and the skies dark. There was a faint sound catching a ride on tonight's wind and if you listened closely, you could hear music. It was a tune that was very familiar and the words go something like this…

When Johnny comes marching home again…Hurrah!

Hurrah! We'll give him a hearty welcome then…

Hurrah! Hurrah! …….

The old sanitarium just off of Stone Street Road was about to take on a new purpose….

www.ingramcontent.com/pod-product-compliance
Lightning Source LLC
LaVergne TN
LVHW051035070526
838201LV00009B/212